A WAY OUT
of the TRAP

A WAY OUT
of the TRAP
A Ten-Step Program for
SPIRITUAL GROWTH

by
Nathan Rutstein

Bahá'í
PUBLISHING
Wilmette, IL 60091

Bahá'í Publishing, 415 Linden Avenue, Wilmette, Illinois 60091-2844
© 2007 by the National Spiritual Assembly of the Bahá'ís of the United States
First edition published 1995. First Bahá'í Publishing edition 2007
All rights reserved. Printed in the United States of America.

10   09   08   07   1   2   3   4

Library of Congress Cataloging-in-Publication Data

Rutstein, Nathan.
    A way out of the trap : a ten-step program for spiritual growth /
by Nathan Rutstein. — 1st Bahá'í Pub. ed.
        p. cm.
    Includes bibliographical references.
    ISBN-13: 978-1-931847-40-7 (alk. paper)
    ISBN-10: 1-931847-40-1 (alk. paper)
        1. Spiritual life—Bahai Faith. I. Title.

BP380.R874 2007
297.9'344—dc22

                                              2007060825

Cover and book design by Suni D. Hannan
Cover photo by Todd Pearson

Contents

Contents

Acknowledgments

It takes more than a writer to produce a published book. First, I am grateful to my editor, Beth Hinshaw, who not only insisted on perfection; she also designed the cover and interior format [of the previous edition].

I am also deeply appreciative to those who critiqued the manuscript. Many of their insights helped in the shaping of the final draft. The reviewers were: Judy Garis, John Hinshaw, Sylvia Kaye, Tom Keedy, Bob and Elaine Milliken, Gary Morrison, Elena Mustakova-Possardt, and Claire Vreeland.

I am most grateful to my wife, Carol, whose struggle to find her true self inspired me to engage in a similar journey. Without that experience, this book could not have been written.

Nathan Rutstein
Amherst, Massachusetts

Introduction

Trying to share a social remedy is difficult if what you offer is unfamiliar and doesn't fit within the established patterns of thinking that most people follow in life. As a result, you hold back. You hold back for fear of alienating someone or being considered unrealistic, or worse yet, fanatical. And there's always the fear of shattering a person's faith. But holding back can be personally painful, especially when you know that what you're holding back can help those who are suffering from what once troubled you.

I can no longer hold back what I know, not when I see such a growing hopelessness all around me, virtually everywhere. Being a writer, I have chosen to break my silence by writing this book. It is an attempt to share with the public a spiritual development process by which spiritually starved women and men can gain the courage, the inner strength, and the guidance needed to break out of the trap we find ourselves in. This process may help us to discover or better understand what we have longed to attain: an understanding of our purpose in life and how to fulfill it.

The first part of the book is a description of this trap and the effect the trap has on us. So many of us refuse to openly acknowledge our entrapment; out of self-defense we create an artificial comfort zone known as denial.

In describing the trap and how it came into being, I relied on the popular media and combed through newspapers and magazines for evidence. It wasn't a difficult task. Every day the evidence was made available through news stories, commen-

1

taries, analysis, and passionate editorials. Radio and television newscasts and documentaries were also used as sources.

For more than a year I was exposed to a blizzard of statistics describing the deterioration of society. It was a staggering experience, especially because I didn't try to lessen the impact of the stories on the first few pages of the newspaper by turning to the funnies or to the sports section. I took note of the evidence of the increase in serious problems such as murder; rape; child molestation; gang violence; white-collar crime; racist acts; unethical practices among business leaders, lawyers, doctors, and clergy; the universal corruption of the spirit; drug addiction and suicide; and the apparent impotence of sacred and social institutions to bring about any lasting improvements. I wasn't alone in thinking that society was in deep trouble. Some respected social and political observers were also pondering the mounting evidence. I could commiserate with nationally syndicated columnist Bob Greene when he cried out in print after reporting how three San Jose, California, teenagers butchered an eight-year-old boy for items worth less than $100: "Unless we can figure out a way to cure the dying national soul, we might as well just turn out the lights and say a prayer on our way out, because it is all over."[1]

In my travels over the years, I have noticed an increase in social apathy and a sort of numbness displayed by the people I have come in contact with. I felt compelled to share with these people the thoughts, feelings, and steps I have taken to help myself emerge from my own stupor. My first impulse was to share all of the evidence I had collected, thinking that unless we are willing to face the critical nature of our condition, we won't be motivated to seek a solution. But after pondering the evidence and consulting with others, I realized that deep down, most people are aware of the condition, but they have given up hope of ever finding a way to change. Because they don't know how to change, they have become obsessed with trying to survive in the least painful way possible. Ignoring the condition seems like the most sensible way of dulling the pain. It became apparent that the best thing I could do was to offer ways to break out of the trap and to describe the benefits in store for those who spring free. But I realized, too, that if we are to keep from being entrapped again, it is important to understand how we become ensnared. In other words, we need to take preventative measures.

Readers will discover that much of what they consider reality isn't real at all. In some respects this experience will be like discarding the wrong map for the right one. Knowing that we are heading in the right spiritual direction will make us more secure. My hope is that readers will find in this book what their spirit has always sought—the way to hope, faith, and the spiritual sustenance that is so necessary to function as a complete human being.

1

Surviving the Self-Made Trap

Normally, I don't read a Sunday newspaper, especially not the encyclopedic *New York Times*. I don't have the time or energy to comb through an avalanche of verbiage. Besides, in the past, when I would purchase a Sunday paper much of it went unread, and I hate to be wasteful.

On the morning of November 13, 1993, I caved in. While waiting to board a plane at Chicago's O'Hare Airport, I checked out the newspaper headlines in the gift shop. The Sunday *Times*' lead story jumped out at me. After reading the first paragraph, I bought the paper. I was moved by what President Bill Clinton told a gathering of clergy at the Memphis church where Dr. Martin Luther King Jr. delivered his last sermon. In reading excerpts of the president's impromptu remarks, I sensed a cry springing from a saddened soul, from a person who understood the source of the violence, crime, racism, and family fracturing that plague our country. But it was obvious that he had no solution. And when he appealed to his audience to help overcome the "great crisis of the spirit that is gripping the American people,"[1] I sensed that he had to be desperate, for the ministers were looking to him to provide what they could not. I was impressed not only by the president's sincerity and compassion, but also by the fact that he was willing to say what so many Americans refuse to acknowledge publicly: America—the last remaining super-power—is fighting for its life.

It doesn't take a scientific study or a grand awakening to acknowledge that humanity is desperately groping for ways to lift itself out of the mess it has created for itself. Every day the media reminds us of the mess. Watching the news on TV is like watching a horror show. Daily newscasts dwell on murder, mayhem in the streets, rape, child molestation, institutional corruption, and the fracturing of the family as a social institution. We witness so much misery that we may begin muttering to ourselves expressions like "The world is going mad; it's an insane asylum." In time, our muttering leads to belief, and we become increasingly frightened. Finally, from deep in our soul we ask, "When will the madness end?"

You would think that people wouldn't watch the news after being exposed to a daily dose of misery. But many do, hoping that one day soon there will be an announcement like the one that declared the Cold War had ended, which sparked a fire of hope within us that soon faded. Most of us will admit that the news of the Soviet Union's unraveling and the end of the Cold War caught us by surprise. So we hope for another surprise and continue to watch, except that most of us are secretly awaiting what we feel would be the ultimate news story: that a way has been found to abolish all war, establish world peace, end poverty, strengthen family and community solidarity, eliminate crime, or find a cure for cancer or AIDS.

While we cling to our wish, we refuse to reveal it in public for fear that it will seem foolish compared to the ideas of distinguished thinkers who, with great certainty, eloquently defend their notion that as long as humans exist there will always be war, crime, poverty, family feuding, and clashes within and among communities. After all, they point out through the finite and imperfect tool of logic, the human being is an animal and is therefore driven by instinct and is subject to "the survival of the fittest." As a consequence, they add, humans will continue to behave as other predators normally do. Yet we continue to gaze at the television as some sort of miracle producer, awaiting a "great announcement." But it doesn't come. Instead, as we watch and listen, our fears are continually reinforced as we grow more informed of humanity's plight.

This doesn't mean that what we long for cannot be realized. As is so often the case, the solution to a baffling problem is so simple that we overlook it and expend considerable energy in explorations that lead us further and further away from the solution. We don't have to go far to find what we need. The solution is within each one of us, waiting to be developed. The nineteenth-century American philosopher Ralph Waldo Emerson said, "What lies behind us and what lies before us are tiny matters compared to what lies within us."[2]

Because most of us haven't found what we yearn for, we find ourselves trapped in a condition that we have unconsciously helped to create. I know what it's like being in the trap. It was an awful feeling. I felt helpless because I couldn't extricate myself from that sense of horror, that sense of hopelessness and the dog-eat-dog atmosphere so pervasive in the social, economic, and political system—all of which, I later learned, constitutes *the trap.* The escape measures I employed, like watching TV, going to movies, and going on vacations, brought only temporary relief. The trap seemed to be everywhere—like smog in the air—and I was contributing to the pollution. Helplessly, I found myself contributing to a debilitating process that I and others had accepted as normal.

In retrospect, I now know why. Out of ignorance and desperation I did what everyone else seemed to be doing in order to survive in a dog-eat-dog atmosphere. I felt I had no alternative but to buy into the trap's code of behavior. In socially rationalized ways, I lied, cheated, and resorted to deception. I was selfish and engaged in gossiping and backbiting whenever I felt it was to my advantage to do so. I was going crazy, but because everyone else around me was in the same condition, I wasn't aware of what was happening to me. We all seemed "normal." At the time, I wasn't aware that my negative thoughts, feelings, attitudes, and behaviors were merging with similar thoughts, feelings, attitudes, and behaviors from almost everyone else in the community, forming a nearly imperceptible network of people possessed of negativity, skepticism, and pessimism. Only when I looked at life and reality from a totally different point of view did I realize that my fears and anxieties affected me and everyone around me—at home, at work, and even at play—and that I was affected on a daily basis by similar feelings harbored by others. This interchange of conscious and unconscious negative feelings is, indeed, a major factor in the formation of humanity's prevailing condition—*the trap!* Our combined fears, anxieties, and sense of hopelessness and horror have created a strange unity between us. We share the same longings, concerns, and fears revolving around personal and community survival in a world growing more and more unpredictable and violent. In essence, the collective consciousness I've described is a web of psychological oppression.

We decry the fact that we find ourselves caught in the web. Our fear is heightened by the fact that no one seems to know why we are ensnared in this web. Deep down we question the theory of the survival of the fittest in relation to humanity. But repeated examples of negative human behavior, even on the part of society's institutions, turn the dominance of an animal nature within us into a perceived norm. This makes it impossible for us to extricate ourselves from the clutches of the silent horror and hopelessness within us and from the dog-eat-dog atmosphere around us. We resort to the only rational thing we can think of: We adjust to the prevailing condition (the trap) in the most painless way possible. Some who have the greatest fear of the pain stoop to unconventional measures. They try to drown the pain in alcohol or numb their sensibilities with other drugs. Others end up in mental hospitals or commit suicide. The majority trudge ahead trying to make the best of a worsening situation, unsure of how to impede its progress. They find themselves in the paradoxical position of contributing to the very development of the collective consciousness they want to break out of. It's not surprising that ninety-five million Americans suffer from some form of drug, alcohol, or tobacco addiction.[3] Millions more are addicted to gambling, sex, food, physical fitness, or their work.

The psychological oppression that afflicts adults plagues youth as well, and often their sense of hopelessness is even more profound because they are less skilled at hiding it from themselves.

In my travels across North America I have sensed youth groping for meaning in life and not having much success in finding it. They want desperately to break out of the trap they feel their elders have created for them. As they flail away, making more commotion than headway in freeing themselves, their condition worsens. To illustrate the gravity of the problems our youth face daily, I must share with you a letter from a seventeen-year-old who poured her heart out to her grandmother, the only adult she trusted. The content of the letter reflects the deep-seated fears, concerns, and longings of many of the youth I have met.

Dear Grandma,

I suspect you know by now why I'm in the hospital and are wondering why I tried to take my life. I can tell you, because you have always listened to what I have had to say. Unfortunately, my parents have never heard me; nor have my teachers. They have always given advice based on what they felt was best for me. But how can you do that when you don't really know the person you are advising? I know my parents are horrified at the thought of their daughter trying to kill herself when she had what they feel every young woman wants—fine clothes, a beautiful home, and her own car. They probably feel I'm ungrateful. The trouble is they don't know what I really want. I have tried to explain, but they discount what I say and instead instruct me on what "sensible people" should want in life.

Grandma, I fear going home. Not because I hate my parents. I just can't take their insistence that I adopt their ways. I prefer staying here. At least at the hospital there's no yelling, no interference with my thinking deeply about what I want, and what I know and don't know.

With the peace and quiet here, I have been able to sort out the craziness at school, which had become something routine for me. I never questioned what was going on there, and the kinds of things we did. It all seemed normal. I think I now know why we behaved the way we did. Guys carried weapons to school as a means of gaining respect. Some girls did too—to be cool. We took drugs and drank beer and vodka to dull the pain that living generated in us. We went wild at rock concerts for the same reason we took dope and drank. We had sex because we wanted to express our independence and try out something exciting before it was too late. Many of us girls, including me, had sex, and deep down we hoped we would get pregnant. You never knew this: when I was fifteen, my wish came true. But Mom and Dad forced me to have an abortion. I wanted a baby badly, because I wanted something that I created, someone I could love who would love me. There are times when I think about my baby and cry.

While I know some things, it's all about the things I have done wrong. There is so much I don't know, stuff that's related to what I want most, and I sense it's important. My behavior in the past was a cry for some understanding, for answers to questions that trouble me. They trouble me because I don't know who to go to for answers. I guess I don't know who to trust. Those who I have approached have disappointed me.

I feel alone in a world that my heart tells me is supposed
to be a home for all life. You see, my head tells me one
thing, but my heart tells me something else. In the hospital
I follow my heart, but outside I'm afraid to. In fact, outside
there's no time to wonder about the universe and what my
relationship to it is, or what the purpose of life is, or who I
really am. Here I can wonder about such things, and ideas
come to me. It doesn't bother me that I don't know if they
are right or wrong. What matters is that I wonder, and getting ideas makes me feel good, and I want to wonder more.
Doing that makes me feel alive and want to live. I begin to
sense who I really am, and what I'm capable of doing. As
long as I can remember, I've never thought of such things.
It's as if I was dead. Grandma, maybe my attempt at suicide
was a desire to become alive.

> Thanks for always listening,
> Linda

2

Fleeing the Trap

My success in gaining my freedom from the trap doesn't mean that I am different or better than others, that I am free of faults or that I possess all of the answers to perplexing questions having to do with human nature and humanity's future. All it means is that I have chosen to move in a different direction—something that everyone can do. In a way, I'm grateful for having been in the trap, because I can empathize with those who remain trapped and grope for a way out. With that knowledge, I can be of some assistance in helping others find their way out. But I have discovered that gaining freedom from the trap doesn't catapult you into a life of permanent ease. The pull of the trap is powerful. To prevent being drawn back, daily effort is required.

At first the effort may seem tortuous. That's understandable, for in the beginning you find yourself in unfamiliar waters, trying to resist the urge to return to the shore, to a familiar place of safety. What straightens out your course is steadfastness and a commitment to develop what you have discovered within you, namely your spiritual reality or true self. In time you gain a different perspective of what a human being is and what the purpose of life is. You develop a healthier attitude in grappling with tests and difficulties. As a result, life becomes a more exciting and joyous adventure. To maintain this state of mind requires continuing effort. To cease the effort is to be drawn back into the trap. A method for developing this understanding and state of mind is described later on in this book.

Finding our way out of the trap enables us to see things about the condition of the world that are not discernible to those who are still captive. What is it that the trapped do not see? Among other things, they don't see that the misery they are experiencing is the result of a destructive process operating in the world—a process that must run its course so we can appreciate that something new is being created by a simultaneous and opposite constructive process. Because they cannot appreciate the great transition taking place in the world, they are unaware that humanity is actually moving forward. All they can see is the increasing pain, misery, mayhem, and the underlying fear of where it will lead.

The two processes functioning simultaneously in human society today are decline and growth: The voids being created by the former are being filled by the latter. In the physical world we can see parallels of these two complementary processes. For example, plants die and decompose to become the nutrients of the next generation. The process of decay is only a stage that must take place before those same physical elements can be incorporated into new forms. Though this dynamic dual process within society is shrouded in chaos, it is, in fact, taking place. With each passing day the pace quickens, and the world's condition—strange as it seems—is growing worse and better at the same time.[1]

Václav Havel, the former president of the Czech Republic, is aware of the processes of decline and growth occurring in the world today. In a speech delivered in Philadelphia in July of 1994, he shared what he has discovered:

There are good reasons for suggesting that the modern age has ended. Many things indicate that we are going through a transitional period, when it seems that something is on the way out and something else is painfully being born. It is as if something were crumbling, decaying and exhausting itself, while something else, still indistinct, was arising from the rubble.[2]

Sadly, the trapped can't see what Havel sees because of their inability to detach themselves from the process of decline. We are witnessing, at an accelerating pace, the crumbling of familiar institutions and cherished ways; trusted forms of government are failing, and it is scary. Fear, a common reaction to the unknown, sets in because we don't know what will replace those institutions and ways of living in which we have invested our faith and placed our trust. The fear obscures our vision of the future and therefore prevents any real hope in the future. As a consequence, it is difficult to notice the process of growth. The trapped have deluded themselves into becoming comfortable with the declining order and, even though it is deteriorating, they have learned to make appropriate adjustments when it sputters and falters. In a way, those who are trapped, out of desperation, have fooled themselves into thinking that the ship is not sinking even though they can see the water level rising.

Once freed from the trap, however, people are able to see things they never saw before, and they gain a perspective of the world's direction that they were incapable of recognizing while trapped. For example, the pain in the world could be viewed as birth pangs. A pregnant humanity is in labor, about to give birth to a global civilization. The more the trapped

resist the delivery process, the more turbulent and painful the birth. Once they have escaped from the trap with their broadened view, those who are free can turn their attention to providing others with encouragement. The freed understand that the tumult and chaos are the result of the breaking up of the cover that has masked society's true condition for a long time. By exploring the development of the field of human psychology in the past fifty years or so, we can appreciate why society's present condition is a necessary phase in the evolution of the human race.

By the midpoint of the twentieth century, more and more people began to turn to psychiatrists and psychologists for guidance about how we should act and think. Sound mental health was viewed as the ability to accept and live by the prevailing mores and social standards. Experts at the time felt that what was normal was being able to conform to the prevailing conditions. They and others were unaware of many of the hidden problems. What mattered most was maintaining outward social structures in the community—preserving the status quo. It didn't matter to those in power that the structures were fundamentally flawed, discriminatory, and unjust. Consequently, considerable energy was channeled into maintaining the socially accepted outward norms within the home and in public. For example, in much of North America and northern Europe, the accepted norm was to avoid any extreme displays of emotions. Breaking from the norm was a sign of weakness. Most knew that to be accepted in society required continual repression of certain instincts. They worked hard at giving the impression of being cool, calm, and collected—always in control. But they

paid a price for their repressed behavior. Over a period of time they evolved into numbed, unimaginative, unquestioning men and women, fearful of change and tradition-bound, valuing the Christmas tree more than the holy day it was supposed to symbolize.

Those who deviated from the norm were considered abnormal, a term many equated with being crazy. As a result, some people repressed impulses that were contrary to the established social norms. Some of those impulses had to do with resisting or wanting to change certain accepted practices and traditions that were blatant injustices, such as racism and sexism. They were repressed because of the hostile way the majority usually reacted to any deviation from the prevailing mores.

Since the 1950s, which many still consider "the good old days," we have become aware of other practices festering beneath the cloak of normalcy: child abuse, child molestation, spousal abuse, alcoholism, institutional corruption, rape, and immoral acts by acknowledged moral exemplars such as clerics and physicians. While many sensed that this sort of thing was going on, they felt powerless to do anything about it. The media, government, educational and industrial leaders, even most of the clerics, gave the impression that everything was fine. Voiceless, the masses made adjustments, forcing themselves to believe the assessment of the powerful and influential people "who always know best."

Today the cloak is being removed, and we find ourselves overwhelmed by a myriad of problems that we pretend don't exist. While we are overcome by the enormity of the challenges that face us in trying to find solutions, some progress is being made toward helping people dismantle the false self they had to develop in order to function acceptably in a world based on pretense and wishful thinking. For the first time, we are exposed to the true condition of society. While it is painful to deal with, this recognition itself represents progress. Imagine where we would be had the cloak not been removed. Knowing the truth puts us in a position to find ways to heal what really ails us.

With the recognition that the world's condition is a part of the reciprocal processes of decay and growth, we can gain more insight into the relationship between the immediate problems around us and the evolutionary flow of humanity as a whole. In other words, it is now possible to see where humanity is heading and, to some degree, to see what's in store for us in the future.

When we begin to look beyond our individual concerns, we can appreciate the results of the current conditions; through this convulsive process humanity is being guided from its collective adolescence to maturity. At the beginning of adolescence, everything revolves around the self. Slowly, and often tumultuously, the individual begins to include relationships with others in the focus of his or her life. The process, beginning with a small group, and often accompanied by the great pathos of failure and success, eventually expands until finally, as a mature adult, the individual understands the necessities and rewards of the interdependence of all human beings. In symbolic terms we can see that humanity is moving away from a kind of adolescent dependence upon a stage of nationhood toward recognition of its membership in an emerging world community, realizing finally that the "earth is but one country, and mankind its citizens."[3]

Of course those who are trapped reject the idea that we are witnessing the internationalization of our planet, citing the unraveling of the Soviet Union and Yugoslavia into smaller, antagonistic nations. Actually, the breakup of the Soviet Union and Yugoslavia was a step toward globalization, for theirs was an artificial union forged by brute force. Today these new nations realize they can't survive without joining a greater geopolitical entity like the European Union. Who would have ever thought during the cold-war era that Russia would one day become a partner to the United States in building a space station? Nations in Southeast Asia, the Caribbean, Africa, and North and South America are also making a voluntary thrust toward unity.

While those who remain trapped grieve over what they perceive as the loss of power in the old world order, evidence of an emerging new world order is mounting. There are international laws regulating fishing, the protection of endangered species, air travel, and communication-satellite traffic, the benefits of which ultimately enhance the well-being of all. There is the emergence of an international system of collective security, and a growing reliance on the United Nations to solve disputes between countries. There is the development of a global economy. Scientists from many countries are working together to eliminate acid rain pollution and to assemble an international space station from which research can be conducted. Although the latest phase of the social, economic, political, and spiritual evolution of humanity is still in its formative stage and is far from being fully developed; nevertheless, there is no turning back, just as there was no reverting from nationhood to tribalism. The internationalization of our planet is the next logical step in the social evolution of humanity.

Those who have been fortunate enough to see our planet from space have been profoundly affected by the experience and clearly see the need for this next logical step. While on a weeklong flight on the space shuttle *Discovery* in June of 1985, the first Arab astronaut in space, Sultan Bin Salman al-Saud of Saudi Arabia, made the following comment: "The first day or so we all pointed to our countries. The third or fourth day we were pointing to our continents. By the fifth day we were aware of only one earth."[4]

3

Overcoming Our Distorted View of Reality

The true nature of reality has to do with what exists: the known, the yet to be discovered, and the unknowable interrelated physical and spiritual processes that sustain the countless aspects of life.

What is known is based on human sense perception and intellectual inquiry, which can lead to the creation and use of advanced technologies. These technologies can help us penetrate some of what our senses cannot perceive. For example, through the electron microscope we can see how human cells function.

Much of what is yet to be discovered will most likely be related to what we think we know in full. In other words, the new discoveries will provide us with greater understanding of the composition and characteristics of what has already been discovered. Take, for example, the basic elements of life. At one time the atom was considered the smallest particle of matter. Then the protons, neutrons, and electrons were discovered. Later scientists discovered the quark, which has the attributes of charm, color, and strangeness. There is always the possibility of discovering some new aspect of reality that has always existed but has eluded the scientific probing of the past.

What constitutes that which is unknowable? The essence of all things, including our Creator. All that science can do is discover, record, and classify the characteristics of things, both visible and invisible.

Although it is impossible for any human being to comprehend the essence of any aspect of reality, there are some thinkers who come close to understanding how the processes within reality are interrelated. The contemporary Buddhist philosopher Thich Nhat Hanh reveals how in his book titled *Being Peace.*

> Just as a piece of paper is the fruit, the combination of many elements that can be called non-paper elements, the individual is made of non-individual elements. If you are a poet, you will see clearly that there is a cloud floating in this sheet of paper. Without a cloud there will be no water; without water, the trees cannot grow; and without trees, you cannot make paper. So the cloud is in here. The existence of this page is dependent on the existence of a cloud. Paper and cloud are so close. Let us think of other things, like the sunshine. Sunshine is very important because the forest cannot grow without sunshine, and we humans cannot grow without sunshine. So the logger needs sunshine in order to cut the tree, and the tree needs the sunshine in order to be a tree. Therefore you can see sunshine in this sheet of paper. And if you look more deeply . . . with the eyes of those who are awake, you see not only the cloud and the sunshine in it, but that everything is here: the wheat that became the bread for the logger to eat, the logger's father—everything is in this sheet of paper.[1]

Most of us, however, haven't developed the penetrative sight of Thich Nhat Hanh. We have an incredibly limited and often distorted view of the most common elements of reality, such as the air we breathe, the planet we live on, and the universe it is a part of, as well as the nature and station of the human being. In fact, much of what we accept as truth isn't true. It is a mishmash of myths, biases, perceptions, fantasies, traditions, and customs that border on superstition, with some superficial smatterings of truth.

Most people rarely explore the nature of reality, spending most of their time reacting to daily stimuli. When pressed to define or describe reality, they often point to the same stimuli that shaped their behavior and beliefs.

Reality often defies logic. When we employ only logic to explain some aspect of reality, we usually fail to unravel the truth. But because our explanation is logical, we assume what we have said or written is the truth.

Why is logic terribly limited in explaining reality? Because paradoxes abound in reality, and a paradox is essentially illogical. Take for example one of the greatest paradoxes: the simultaneous operation of two mighty processes—entropy and evolution, which operate as opposing forces. Entropy has to do with the degradation or winding down of all things physical, including our planet and everything on it—and that includes our bodies. Nothing we do can prevent our bodies from eventually ceasing to function.

While evolution has to do with refined development of every object within entropy's clutches, it is also a spiritual force of growth. The more humanity matures spiritually, the less animallike the body appears. Human beings have always been human beings and not animals, despite their different shapes and forms in the distant past.[2] (More on what distinguishes human beings from animals will be discussed in later chapters.) Through the ages the human beings' apelike appearance faded as they grew more conscious of their spiritual capacity and became involved in its development. Their brains expanded, their minds sharpened, they grew more creative and exhibited more and more virtues. Chances are that had humanity failed to discover its spiritual capacity, today's human being would be just another predator in the jungle of life.

Upon deep reflection, many of us would most likely discover that much of the prevailing view of reality was conceived by respected authorities or experts and promoted by their zealous followers as the truth.

For example, though subatomic particles existed during the heyday of ancient Greece, Aristotle wasn't aware of them. He believed that matter was comprised of only four elements: air, earth, water, and fire. He and some other classical Greek thinkers also believed that our planet was stationary and that the sun revolved around it.[3] This is only one example in history of how we have been misled by a prevailing authority into believing that reality is what the senses perceive or the mind reasons. In truth, reality springs from a dynamic pattern whose origin and essence are a mystery.

If we don't understand the way the pattern functions, we will remain in the trap, still believing in the misconceptions of reality that were hailed as truth by respected authorities of the past. An example can be seen in the tonsil removal craze that swept over America in the 1930s and 1940s: Leading physicians promoted the procedure as a preventive medical step until they discovered that the human tonsil had a legitimate purpose in combating disease.

A particularly horrendous study, done in good faith by a renowned Swedish botanist, physician, and zoologist in the 1700s, was a contributing factor to the development of modern racism. Carolus Linnaeus, who is known as the father of modern taxonomy, classified thousands of animal and plant species in his lifetime and also broke down the human species into four "distinct" groups based on skin color. For example, he described American Indians as reddish, choleric, obstinate, contented, and regulated by customs; Europeans as white, fickle, sanguine, blue-eyed, gentle, and governed by laws; Asians as sallow, grave, dignified, avaricious, and ruled by opinions; and Africans as black, phlegmatic, cunning, lazy, lustful, careless, and governed by caprice. Though Linnaeus had very limited personal experience with three of "the four families of man" and his ideas on this subject have been throughly debunked, his thinking was embraced by the nineteenth-century anthropological community, which, in turn, influenced the thinking of people today, including scientists. Linnaeus's observations of what would later be called the races of man were based largely on assumptions and sketchy data related to him by European travelers to Africa, Asia, and the Americas.[4]

Some of the illusions that are still prominent among many of the trap-dwellers include the following: The universe is like a huge machine; Earth is the center of the universe; whites are inherently superior to people of color; blacks, whites, Chinese, American Indians, Irish, Italians, and in fact all ethnic groups are different species; the human being is a body with a soul; the devil and original sin are real.

Over the years, academic and religious myopia, as well as
economic and political shortsightedness, greed, and at times
arrogance, led to the perpetuation of these illusions as fundamental truths. This energy led to the institutionalization
of barriers that made it difficult for people to legitimately
question the efficacy of established views. The process employed by many clerics and educators to gain an understanding of reality can be compared to peering through a keyhole
to capture the full grandeur and beauty of a sunset. They
had to resort to imagination in order to explain what they
could not see. Unfortunately, philosophies and scientific theories that still influence our thinking resulted from this "keyhole" investigation of reality.

To gain a broader and more penetrative view of reality, it
is necessary to explore not only the composition of a human
being, but also the composition of the human race, our
planet, and our universe. There is still so much more to uncover. Modern science has gained a greater understanding of
how many of the different aspects of reality are supposed to
relate to one another—the physical and spiritual, the individual and community, even the cells within our body. Unfortunately, most of us remain unaware of this knowledge,
especially the principle of interrelatedness, and we continue
to embrace the illusion of separateness. Every living thing on
earth and elsewhere, from a microbe to a human being, is an
interconnected aspect of an organically expanding universe
so immense that no one is able to measure it.

In recent years, a few profound thinkers have helped to enlighten us about our relationship to our planet and its relationship to the rest of creation. Through their vision we have
been able to see things we never saw before and replace old,

inaccurate notions with a fresh understanding of the basic processes that have been in operation ever since life appeared on earth. Even the most learned of past generations could not conceive of what we are now able to see.

A great visionary of our times, architect and philosopher R. Buckminster Fuller, opened the eyes of some of us to aspects of reality that had previously escaped our narrowly focused vision of the world. In describing our planet as a spaceship, he altered a core feeling within us that we live on a massive, static, big rock within a cluster of other rocks that our elementary school textbooks called the solar system. Our science teachers told us that the Earth revolved around the Sun, but somehow that image never registered, never became a part of our consciousness. Our imagination was earthbound. From a sensory level, we accepted as reality the Sun's rising and setting each day. Fuller, however, dashed that illusion by stirring our imagination with imagery that made us appreciate the fact that we are all passengers on "Spaceship Earth," on a continuous journey around a star we call the Sun. It takes 365 and a quarter days to revolve around the Sun, a process that has been going on for billions of years. It's amazing that most of us go to sleep each night without ever wondering whether Spaceship Earth's journey will continue and what would happen if it didn't. What faith!

Through Fuller's vision we were reminded that in our everyday lives we are conscious of only a very limited sense of reality. We live and function and make decisions based on information that we can see, hear, and touch. For centuries, scientists had observed the visible world around us and carefully categorized all its parts and their interrelationships. It was a very limited understanding of the relationships that eventually led science and philosophy to see nature as a kind of machine, even living organisms were considered mechanical, with each part performing its special function. The scientist was always creating tools and instruments that could take us beyond our unaided senses. The natural extension of our understanding was that the world beyond our senses was also part of the machine. "Like human-made machines," states Fritjof Capra in *The Turning Point*, "The cosmic machine was thought to consist of elementary parts. Consequently it was believed that complex phenomena could always be understood by reducing them to their basic building blocks and by looking for the mechanisms through which they interacted. This attitude, known as reductionism, has become so deeply ingrained in our culture that it has often been identified with the scientific method."[5]

But astronomers are now finding that the universe is an ongoing dramatic event. Within this boundless body of fluctuating energy that is continually changing and moving exist countless galaxies, each with hundreds of millions of stars and, presumably, many planets. What we think of as outer space isn't a dormant place; new stars and planets are continually developing and disintegrating. In the vast distances between all of the celestial bodies, there are not voids as our senses lead us to believe, but instead great fields of energy composed of subatomic particles, atoms, and molecules, spinning about at lightspeed, too small to be seen with even the most powerful telescopes, let alone the naked eye.

"Today," Capra adds, "the universe is no longer seen [by some scientists] as a machine, made up of a multitude of separate objects, but appears as a harmonious indivisible whole; a network of dynamic relationships that include the human observer and his or her consciousness in an essential way."[6] Physicist James Jeans also describes this phenomenon: "Today there is a wide measure of agreement . . . that the stream of knowledge is heading towards a non-mechanical reality; the universe begins to look more like a great thought than a giant machine."[7] But we don't live in outer space yet, so how do these new insights into the universe relate to us here on the surface of our planet?

Through Fuller's vision we are reminded of the limitations of our perceptions of the world. The terms "up" and "down" are an example. We all understand these terms as they relate to our experiences living on the plane of our planet, but considering what man understands of the nature of the universe and the Earth's place in it, there is a great deal more than just up and down. Considering the Earth's place in the universe (wherever that may be), saying that we are looking up at the sky, in reality, is incorrect. If you follow that logic, then the Australian must be looking down at the sky, but Australia really isn't "down under." Actually, what he is doing is looking *out* at the sky. From a universal perspective, directions such as north, south, east, and west are also meaningful only in a relative sense; that is, when you are standing in one place on a two-dimensional plane. When looking at the moving planet on television from a vantage point out in space, east becomes west at some point and west becomes east. What were clear and simple ideas of the world around us are now slowly being understood from different points of view.[8]

Another visionary, perhaps the world's leading communications philosopher in his day, Marshall McLuhan, understood these limited ways of perceiving the world and startled many people decades ago when he called our planet "a glo-

bal village." He saw that originally the earth was free of political, economic, social, and religious barriers; that with advancements in technology such as computers and television,
these man-made barriers would eventually crumble and that
people who lived apart would interact regularly. Eventually,
this association would lead to the adoption of new moral
values, and people would learn to care for one another. In
essence, McLuhan saw humanity's destiny—a united human
family living in one country called Earth.

Today, with the emergence of a global economy and the communications satellites that can bring every event throughout the
world to our television sets, more of us are beginning to see and
feel, at least in part, what McLuhan saw and felt. Even in places
such as Bosnia, Cambodia, Rwanda, Haiti, Northern Ireland,
and Somalia, which have been devastated by war and the effects
of prejudice, inequality, and ignorance, we see increasing signs
of hope. Who would have ever thought that apartheid would
end in South Africa in our lifetime, and, even more remarkable,
that a black man would be elected president of that nation?

The United Nations is beginning to search for new ways
of gaining strength by getting more nations involved in solving the world's problems. More and more countries now see
that only an international collective response can cure the
social and political diseases afflicting the human condition.
But reaching this stage on humanity's path toward its destiny has not come about easily or swiftly.

Throughout the centuries there have been many aspects
of reality of which humanity has been unaware. Our planet,
for example, was viewed at one time by even the most learned
and pious as both flat and the center of the universe. Now
we know better, thanks to the vision of a few courageous

philosophers and scientists. Today the roundness of the earth is universally accepted. What's more important is that this acceptance demonstrates that human beings are capable of grasping aspects of reality that even the most erudite people of previous generations didn't grasp—not that those in the past didn't have the capacity to do so.

When I gaze at the live television portrait of our planet in space, I am at peace. I am in awe to think that I am at a place where I exist, where about six billion other human beings exist along with billions of other creatures all busy doing something, even though from this vantage point in space there is no visible human activity. The more I look at this vision of the entire planet, the more I realize that it was meant to be a center of harmony and order. While reflecting on our planet, our solar system, and the little I know of the universe, I wonder how anyone could believe that it all resulted from a chain of accidental physical reactions. To believe this is like accepting the idea that one's set of *Encyclopædia Britannica* resulted from an explosion in a printing press. Could it be that planet Earth in its relation to countless other celestial bodies is the creation of an invisible hand? Everywhere we turn there are evidences of its order, balance, and continuity throughout time that we have usually taken for granted. I marvel over the fact that for millions of years the oxygen level of the Earth's atmosphere has remained constant—at about 21 percent—and that its oceans' salt content has stayed at 3.4 percent.[9] "The atmosphere in fact binds together all of life on earth," says science writer Guy Murchie in *The Seven Mysteries of Life*, "including life in the deep sea, which breathes oxygen (and some air) constantly. And the water of the sea is another of life's common denominators noticeable in the salty flavor of our blood, sweat and tears."[10]

By thinking of the devastation that would result from any change in the air and water, even to a minute degree, I grow grateful to the force that has created and maintains such a remarkable balance. It's as if a thermostat functions within our planet and a power higher than any human being is at the controls. The more I gaze at the resplendent sight of this blue pearl in the sky, the more I realize I am being exposed to an extraordinary message: Within the infinity of the universe, it is the whole planet that is our real home, our only home. It is a single entity whose oneness is to be appreciated and preserved. Whatever disturbances and divisions we find on our planet stem from our lack of understanding that it is a single entity. A limited perception of the world around us results in borders, and even those borders that were made to protect us begin to feel like barriers.

What becomes more and more evident is the need for a worldwide campaign to remove all the man-made barriers that keep human beings apart. I believe the preservation of our planet depends on a higher, shared vision of the interconnectedness of the human family.

I am reminded of a quotation shared by an eminent paleontologist and Jesuit priest, Pierre Teilhard de Chardin, whose understanding of the universe was uniquely shaped by a balance of scientific recognition and religious conviction: "Nothing is precious except that part of you which is in other people and that part of others which is in you. Up there on high, everything is one."[11]

Imagine how much healthier the world would be if the great majority of humankind saw what Teilhard de Chardin saw, took it to heart, and then put it into practice. Many of the animosities that keep peoples and nations apart wouldn't exist. Women and men everywhere would understand the necessity of continually strengthening the bonds that keep the human family together. In essence, Teilhard de Chardin saw what McLuhan saw—humanity's potential to follow a dynamic, divine pattern for creating a global civilization in which all human beings recognize their familial connection with each other. Why were they able to see what most of us haven't seen? They had a clearer understanding of an important aspect of reality and saw the structure of creation. They recognized that our planet, with its dynamic web of interrelated systems, is a relatively insignificant physical element within the universe, functioning as a microscopic cell that houses many smaller cells, including humanity and its nearly six billion cells called human beings. And within each one of them are even smaller cells, sixty to seventy trillion of them, all unique, with a degree of intelligence and interconnectedness. But it doesn't stop there. There are tinier life-forms in the cells within us, molecules that are made up of atoms that are composed of subatomic particles, so small that compared to an atom, a single particle is like a grain of salt somewhere in a 100-story skyscraper. Though all of the cells on earth are interconnected, they don't necessarily adjoin one another. The cells of the tip of our nose don't touch the cells of our big toe, yet, in reality, they are connected: They are connected by intercellular communications through the nervous system and the endocrine system. They are partners in a cellular chain that's programmed to keep the much larger organism—the human being—alive and healthy.

We know that damaged links of any chain will adversely affect the chain's usefulness and in some instances spark disasters. Take the human body, for example. When a cluster of cells within it malfunctions, cancer can result. The same thing can happen to the cell called humanity. When its body is riddled with malfunctioning human beings, a social cancer erupts in the form of dysfunctional communities and societies.

What follows? The cancer spreads, affecting other parts of the greater cell that humanity is a part of—our planet. How? The dysfunctional communities produce dirty air, dirty water, polluted oceans, diminishing rain forests, the annihilation of animal and plant species, violence, famine, drug addiction, alcoholism, diseases, family breakup, racism, moral breakdown, and a state of hopelessness—the kind of condition that presently plagues much of the world.

Every human being is endowed with the capacity to discover and understand the structure of creation. By gaining an understanding of the principle of the oneness of humankind, we gain an understanding of where we fit within the structure of creation. And by gaining a clearer understanding of what a human being is, we gain a clearer understanding of what our responsibilities are in following the dynamic pattern within that structure.

The structure of creation can be likened to a house; the dynamic pattern, to the way we are meant to live in the house. Rejection or a distorted view of the pattern can result in feuding between the dwellers and the partitioning of the house into separate hostile units. But when the dwellers are unified, the house becomes a home.

STEP ONE *Oneness*

4

Understanding the Principle of the Oneness of Humankind

Science recognizes that there are millions of species on earth and that the human species *(Homo sapiens)* is the most sophisticated one. No dolphin or chimpanzee, however clever it may seem, has created a transistor radio or walked on the moon.

What distinguishes the human being from an ape is the power of ideation, the ability to be conscious of our consciousness, free will, and our spiritual dimension. This doesn't mean, however, that there is no linkage between *Homo sapiens* and other life forms. All are aspects of a single reality linked by an invisible chain. All are involved in a continuous interchange of atoms—primarily through breathing. With each breath, every human being inhales and exhales trillions of atoms. (The average human takes approximately ten million breaths a year.)[1] This worldwide exchange of atoms not only involves the atoms of the living from every section of the world, but the atoms of the people of the past, as well as our planet's animals and plant life.

While all species have different capacities and functions, they all share some similar qualities. For example, the power of attraction, which keeps the atoms of a rock together, exists in humans; the plant, like the rock, possesses the power of attraction, plus powers of growth and reproduction, which are evident in man; the animal contains the qualities of the rock and plant, as well as sensory powers and consciousness, which we all possess.

Unfortunately, there are still many people who confuse race with species. They believe that blacks and whites, Chinese and Malays, and all other ethnic groups are separate species. Interbreeding between these groups is the greatest proof that they are members of the same species. A black Nigerian and white Norwegian can produce a child; a human and an ape cannot. Two different *species* cannot produce an offspring that is fertile.

Actually, some of the most prominent geneticists (Haldane, Dobzhansky, and Huxley) agree that all human beings, regardless of geographical location, skin color, or hair texture, are related to one another. We are at most fiftieth cousins. That's right! The Hasidic Jews in Jerusalem, the Inuit in Alaska, the Chinese, the Italians, the Russians, the Nigerians, the Micronesians, a white Anglo-Saxon industrialist from Greenwich, Connecticut, the Pope, and all the kings and queens in the world are cousins.[2]

And you don't have to be a genius to figure this out. Simple arithmetic will do. Double the number of your ancestors for each generation, says Guy Murchie. As you compute backward (consistently multiplying them by two) your personal pedigree would cover humankind before the thirtieth generation (this calculation takes into consideration that we have shared relatives that wouldn't be counted more than once.) In other words, you are related to some Africans, Chinese, Arabs, Malays, American Indians, and Europeans who lived on our planet in the thirteenth century. Go back further to the eighth century, and your ancestors would include all the

Africans, Chinese, Malays, American Indians, Europeans, and everyone else on earth at the time.[3]

When we go beyond the limited perception of our own five senses and use scientific tools, we can expand and refine our understanding. Despite some people's insistence that their blood hasn't been "tainted," there is no such thing as a pure race. In fact, there is no scientific category of "race" at all. The genetic markers supposedly dividing the human species into races represent only a minute fraction of our genetic endowment. The difference between "races" involves a few superficial physical characteristics that have come about because of long-term adaptation to various climates. Furthermore, the boundary between different "races" is not well defined. No matter how one tries to divide humanity into "races," there are always many peoples who do not fit neatly into any of the categories. This is because movement and mixing has always occurred, causing genetic material to pass between widely separated human populations. Even the whites of Dutch extraction, who were the architects of South African apartheid, have an average of 7 percent "nonwhite" genes, according to the calculations of immunologist Dr. N. C. Botha, himself a white of Dutch ancestry.[4]

Over the millennia the mixing has drawn all of the planet's people closer together. Dr. John Woodall of Harvard's School of Medicine points out that genetically, every human being is at least 97 percent similar. Of the 3 percent difference, more than 85 percent of genetic diversity occurs within the same ethnic group. For example, a black is more similar genetically to a white than whites are to each other. The same is true of two blacks.[5]

One might wonder how there could be such a mix of genes when groups of people were separated by mountain ranges and oceans for so long. It is estimated that even during prehistoric times the average person traveled about 250 miles in her lifetime. In their travels, men and women of different groups mated. And there always were the adventurers. For example, the Celts, Phoenicians, Polynesians, and Vikings explored the Americas before the English, French, Portuguese, or Spanish did.[6] They undoubtedly encountered native women and men. The Moors, many of whom were black, visited the British Isles and Ireland. So did the Romans. The Dutch, who were mobile merchants, spread their seed in Asia, Africa, and the Americas. Even the descendants of the Mayflower pilgrims, many of whom became spice traders, were sexually prolific as well in ports in China, India, and Africa; and there were also the secret sexual involvements with American Indians. In America's southland, white plantation masters and mistresses were involved in a two hundred-year-old underground practice of sexual liaisons with their black slaves. This resulted in a wide spectrum of brown, tan, and yellow-skinned "unofficial" offspring, most of whom ended up as blacks, while some passed as whites. According to *The Ohio Journal of Science,* about 155,000 "Negroes" passed over the color line to become "whites" between 1941 and 1950.[7]

There is strong evidence of prehistoric interracial mixing of genes. Archaeologists have found the remains of black, white, and yellow groups living as neighbors in southern France 25,000 years ago. Yet the people living in the same area today consider themselves white.[8]

Even though all humans are related to one another, most of us find this concept difficult to accept, mainly because people in different parts of the world look so different. How, wonders a blond, blue-eyed, fair-skinned Scandinavian, can I be related to a mahogany-brown African? It is possible for the same reason a white and black horse can produce a colt. Both belong to the same species. What causes different skin color and physical features? People living in a particular area for a long time adapt to environmental challenges. Darker skin pigmentation evolved in warmer climates because it is necessary for filtering out excess ultraviolet sunlight and controlling the synthesis of vitamin D.

Humanity can be likened to a majestic tree. The parts that make up the tree are all different, yet all are dependent on one another. Without the branches, twigs, fruits, and leaves, there would be no tree; and even among the different parts there are differences. For example, there are no two branches that are exactly alike; there are no two twigs that are exactly alike; nor are there any leaves that are exactly alike. Yet they are all part of a whole—the tree receives nourishment from one set of roots and from the same sun that nourishes all other trees.

The tree exemplifies the principle of unity in diversity. So does the human body. All of our organs are different from each other, each performing a unique function that the others cannot perform. Yet this diversity is the very basis of a coordinated and healthy life system for the organism. In this sense, diversity is a prerequisite to achieving a whole that is more than the sum of its parts. The principle of unity in diversity is as real as the law of gravity.

Imagine what life would be like if every rock were the same size, weight, color, and shape, if all vegetables tasted alike, if every flower had the same scent, and if every person thought, felt, and walked alike. Such uniformity is unthinkable.

5

Understanding the Nature of a Human Being

There is no greater tragedy today than not understanding our true nature as human beings and thus not functioning the way we were meant to function. To those who are aware of humankind's true nature and spiritual potential, humanity's present condition is a source of sadness.

Several years ago, while I was on a lecture tour in the United Kingdom, I witnessed the reaction of a group of people who, possibly for the first time, heard about what a human being really is. I met these people at a job skills development center in an industrial suburb of Liverpool. I had been asked to give an inspirational talk emphasizing a religious theme. When I met those I was going to address, I realized that they weren't in the mood for religion. The people in the audience, men and women ranging from age eighteen to sixty-five, were unemployed, on welfare, angry, and without hope of extricating themselves from their present condition. Their demeanor and speech revealed that they felt trapped. Their routine of life was the same as that of their parents and grandparents. It consisted of getting a job in one of the town's factories, having as many children as possible, keeping up with their favorite soccer team, and spending time at the local tavern. It seemed that they had no inclination, no interest in even considering the question of what a human being is. They seemed to be victims of a distorted view of reality, unconsciously consenting captives of the trap.

Most of them had given up on the religion of their forefathers and were leaning toward Marxism, a philosophy openly espoused by the center's young, restless, and frustrated university trained instructors. I had the feeling that, had I appeared with a long beard, dressed in a robe and wielding a sword, asking them to join me in breaking into the prime minister's residence in London, they would have followed me enthusiastically.

What was I to talk to them about? In a flash, the thought of speaking to them about what a human being really is came to mind. It felt right, and it proved to be right.

At first I had doubts because many members of the audience seemed skeptical. Some even seemed hostile; however, about halfway through the talk many of them seemed genuinely interested. They were so interested that what was to be a thirty-minute talk stretched into three hours.

They were so fascinated with the information I shared with them that they urged me to return the following day. Unfortunately, I couldn't. I had to be in a different town. For me it was terribly frustrating, for I sensed that they were experiencing a hope that had eluded them throughout their lives up to that point. And I knew, as they did, that a day or two after my talk their newfound hope would fade, and they would revert to their old habits of thinking and behaving.

I never forgot those people—especially their expressions of hope and then disappointment when I had to leave and was unable to refer them to someone else in their city who could amplify what I had shared with them. Somehow I felt that they had a sense of what life would be like if they had the opportunity to study and internalize what I had shared with them. One meeting simply was not enough.

The present state of the world is, by and large, a reflection of our lack of understanding of who we are as human beings. Consequently, we are out of touch with our true reality. It is that simple, but getting people to understand and believe it seems impossible. In a way, it is like trying to persuade a lifelong cave dweller that there are advantages to living and working outside of his cave. Because he has adjusted to his limited surroundings and feels safe, he's emotionally committed to staying where he is. It doesn't matter that he has never gazed into the daylight sky, that passers-by have told him about some of the wonders outside his cave or about the opportunities to learn more about himself and his purpose in life. He remains in the bowels of the cave, determined not to jeopardize his security by venturing out.

If we really knew the potential love and inner beauty that all of us possess, just waiting to be developed, and if we knew our true purpose in life, our world would be a more secure and peaceful place. Our planet would be inhabited by people who are more compassionate than callous, more selfless than selfish, more loving than hateful, more cooperative than competitive, and the human family would be united—a condition I'm sure most people believe is impossible.

There would be no need for missile manufacturing plants, for smart bombs and stealth bombers, or Tomahawk missiles. Humanity would enjoy real peace, not some shaky truce that its framers only hope will last awhile. The seeds of world peace exist within every human heart. Disarmament treaties are important, but there is no greater safeguard of human happiness and prosperity than for people to possess a stronger desire to love rather than hate, a greater desire to trust than to distrust. These and other positive human virtues are the only true insurance against the breaking of treaties. I believe there is no greater challenge today than for humans to look for the good within themselves and others—those unique qualities that set them apart from the beasts of the field—and dedicate themselves to developing those qualities.

Of all living things, only human beings have the capacity to understand that the planet they live on is so tiny that, in reality, it is physically insignificant relative to the rest of the universe. The seal and falcon, for example, are unaware of the universe and our planet's size, place, and function within it. While animals sense the physical world around them, only human beings are aware of their own consciousness; and, unlike animals, humans have the potential to know that other humans are living in different regions of the world. Monkeys in India are not aware of the monkeys in Africa. Our uniqueness as a species is reflected in the dynamic configuration of physical and spiritual aspects that make up human nature. The nature of this configuration requires continuous development if we are to function as complete and mature human beings. By complete and mature, I don't mean perfect, but rather, balanced—a person who is making steady progress both spiritually and physically.

Physically, humans are in many respects no match for animals. On a one-to-one basis and unarmed, we are incapable of vanquishing a tiger or shark in its own environment. We don't possess the strength of a gorilla or an elephant, and we are unable to fly unaided. But we humans can create an airplane and fly faster, higher, and longer than an eagle; we can build a submarine and explore more of the ocean floor than a shark can. While an elephant can crush a village hut, humans can construct skyscrapers and demolish them with man-made dynamite.

While most animals have brains, the human brain is unique. One of its distinguishing characteristics is its cerebral cortex, which processes thought, speech, and memory. Without it, humans would be unable to create airplanes, submarines, build skyscrapers, explore outer space, or discover the solar system within an atom.

Contrary to popular belief, the human brain is not the same thing as the mind. In fact, the mind is actually an aspect of the soul. The brain is an organ in the human body that functions as a central control mechanism to receive, store, and transmit messages from the mind. Consequently, a damaged brain is unable to reflect the full capacity of the mind, much like a faulty lamp transmits a dim or flickering light.

Built into the physical aspect of human nature, which includes the brain, are two important instincts that are necessary for human existence: sex and survival. Without the drive for sex and the drive for survival, humanity would become extinct. Both instincts are natural to us because they are part of our "animal," or physical, nature. However, the difference between humans and apes, which are entirely animal in nature, is that apes lack a soul and are completely governed by physical instincts.

As humans, we are not completely regulated by our physical instincts because we possess a free will, which is an element of the soul. However, we can choose to reject or ignore our spiritual nature and can allow ourselves to become obsessed with sex and survival. When enough people in a community are functioning at such a level, the community becomes dysfunctional, and institutions of society such as marriage and the family break down.

If not guided and controlled by the soul, human instincts and emotions can cause considerable damage. Take anger and greed for example. When a spiritually underdeveloped person becomes angry, he or she could wound or kill someone or turn into a tyrant. Yet a spiritually developing person who feels anger will use it to fight for justice. A spiritually underdeveloped person whose greed-instinct is unchecked will exploit, even hurt others in the effort to amass material wealth, while the spiritually developing person will seek to acquire more virtues and knowledge.

Tragically, many communities around the world are beset by horrific social and economic problems, most of them resulting from spiritual underdevelopment or imbalance. When heavily financed and carefully planned private or public programs, including religious campaigns, fail to solve the problems, a sense of hopelessness results. When this happens, even the efforts of well-meaning social activists and evangelists cannot prevent us from becoming slaves to our physical impulses. This is most apparent when we find ourselves facing severe daily pressures. We may feel we have no alternative but to accept the prevailing attitudes and mores. When we rely primarily on physical instincts to make decisions in our daily lives, we deprive ourselves of the moderating influence of the soul. When we ignore the soul, we allow ourselves to be unduly influenced by all of the competing materialistic stimuli around us. We become preoccupied with survival—whether this means saving our job, saving our house from foreclosure, keeping on top of our bills, or staying one step ahead of our competitors. We are driven by the fight-or-flight stress response, which springs from the physical aspect of our nature.

Deep down we are in pain, confused, wandering in the paths of delusion, at times crying out, often silently, for some form of deliverance—even a miracle. Sadly, many of us try to cure our emotional traumas with physical remedies. We know that a hot fudge sundae, a new car, or a mink coat only bring temporary pleasure. Yet we pursue them anyway, and when the pain returns, our immediate reaction is to eat more hot fudge sundaes and acquire more things. In the end, if we continue to ignore our spiritual nature, the pain is intensified and complicated by pangs of guilt.

Some who sense that a spiritual remedy is required search in darkness, not knowing what to look for. They usually gravitate toward whatever popular spiritual discipline promises some immediate relief or seems to make some rational sense. They may find themselves running away from all of the world's "evils." In time, they find themselves isolated in the cocoon of self-absorption, concerned primarily with satisfying their own needs, deaf to the cries of the community's needy.

This is not spirituality. Unfortunately, traditional organized religion has failed in large measure to guide us toward discovering and developing our spiritual potential, concentrating instead on perpetuating a guise of spirituality in the form of celebrating holy days, organizing festivals, establishing weekly social or recreational activities, performing rituals, and carrying out fund-raising campaigns.

A major reason for the clergy's emphasis on outward religious forms is, I believe, a lack of authentic spiritual development, and that lack is due to an inadequate understanding of the soul. This inadequate understanding on the part of clergy has in turn left followers through the centuries with an incomplete understanding of the nature of the soul, its powers and qualities, its function, its relationship with the body, and the way to truly develop it. Believers in the past were expected simply to accept the existence of the soul on faith. As a result there is a great deal of confusion about what the soul is.

So, what exactly is the soul? While most of us will agree that it has to do with something good, its origin and essence mystify us. We associate it with physical things that we respect, admire, even love, such as "soul food" or "soul music." A television advertisement attempts to describe the "soul" of an automobile in order to impress viewers with the car's beauty and durability. Even best-selling self-help books that try to explain the soul only add to the confusion. Over the years the misconceptions have proliferated, becoming a formidable obstacle to grasping the nature and purpose of the soul. Sadly, our understanding of this most important aspect of human nature seems more confused than ever.

Today, however, there is a glimmer of hope. As the human race approaches the threshold of its maturity, greater knowledge of the soul is, for the first time, available to everyone. This has been made possible through our Creator's intervention with specific guidance about the spiritual development of human beings. (The form this divine intervention has taken will be explored in a later chapter.) New technologies have been created to explore the inner space of one's self. New, spiritually based psychologies have evolved that can help us discover our souls, or true selves. Most people are not aware of this new knowledge and haven't taken the time to explore it, but we will.

When we become aware of the spiritual aspect of our nature—the soul—and we recognize what it is, we discover a way out of the trap. One of the reasons there has been so much emphasis on the development of the physical aspect of our nature instead of the spiritual aspect is because of our lack of understanding of what constitutes the soul and our lack of information about how to develop it.

When we are no longer slaves to the promptings of our physical nature, we can acquire a broader, more penetrative vision, which enables us to understand humanity's destiny and our responsibilities in fulfilling it. Armed with such knowledge, life acquires a higher meaning and purpose, for we see and hear things we never saw or heard before, making us more sensitive to the needs and aspirations of others. Survival becomes necessary so that we might become a greater servant and lover of our fellow human beings and a force for unity wherever we may be. In time, we realize that by following the dictates of the soul, we are contributing to the development of a spiritually centered world civilization. Unaware of the soul and its needs, we remain unable to participate in this divine enterprise and true happiness eludes us.

Happiness, we learn, is growing spiritually and thereby drawing closer to our Higher Power. This doesn't mean achieving physical closeness, nor does it mean fully understanding the essence of the Creative Force, but it does have to do with becoming more dependent upon that Force in negotiating all phases of life. This is what spirituality is all about. If we have not made a conscious connection with our Creator, we cannot function as spiritual beings. It doesn't matter how much money we have given to the church, synagogue, mosque, or temple, nor how often we attend worship services, nor whether we have been officially confirmed. Without making this spiritual connection, we will be like a lamp that's not plugged into its power source.

To make this all-important connection with our Higher Power doesn't require a theology degree, and being a monk or nun or having a member of the clergy point the way does not give us any advantage. Perhaps in the past there was a need for priestly assistance, but in this day when spiritual knowledge abounds and is available to all, any sincere seeker can find the pathway to spiritual growth. Making an unfettered and sustained personal search is important, because when we discover something precious, we develop a passionate ownership of what we find. This kind of emotion makes for true believers who are involved in ongoing personal spiritual development. From such effort springs a genuine desire to grow even more so that we might be more effective in helping to improve the quality of life in our community without being deterred by the pain and suffering around us as we carry out our sincere desire to serve others. This can't be done today by isolating ourselves from society. Our challenge today is to function as developing, conscious, spiritual beings in a society that is dominated by materialistic forces.

When we grow spiritually, we notice that giving becomes a more powerful instinct than taking; love becomes a more comfortable emotion than hatred; we notice, too, that people of all strata of society, including atheists, are drawn to us. They sense something that makes them feel good. At first they may not understand what that good feeling is. All they know is that they like what they feel and want to experience more of it. If they are open-minded, in time they may realize that this particular good feeling comes from discovering their soul.

No one is born expressing the unqualified love and compassion that springs from our souls. Before those qualities can be manifested on a regular basis, they must become an integral part of our character, and for that to happen an understanding of the source of those qualities must be established.

Søren Kierkegaard, a nineteenth-century Danish philosopher and theologian who was extremely controversial in his day, shed light on why spiritual growth is essential. His insights are more appreciated today than when they were first published or shared from the pulpit. In his book *Sickness Unto Death*, Kierkegaard distinguished between depression and despair. Depression, he pointed out, is a quality that often results from external stimuli such as loss of a loved one, losing a job, or serious illness; despair is a self-perpetuating sickness of the soul. One of the symptoms of despair is a lack of consciousness of being a soul.[1]

A person can experience joy from time to time and can be professionally successful yet still suffer from despair. It usually manifests itself when we sense that something is missing from our lives and the search to find it has been fruitless. Perhaps we have tried buying a new car or going on a cruise to an exotic place and have found that this wasn't the answer, though it may have generated a few moments of pleasure.

When we aren't aware of our souls, we don't realize that the nagging internal feeling so often described as anxiety is really the soul crying out to be recognized and developed.

Every person has a soul, but it has to be discovered and developed if it is to be of any value and do what it was meant to do. Not developing our souls is like not turning on a lamp and simply trying to make do in the darkness, which can lead to despair. The soul is the animating force of a human being. When the body is disassociated from the soul at the point of death, the body becomes as rigid as a statue for a few days, then grows limp as decay sets in. The animating force that makes the human being speak, walk, and think is no longer associated with the body that's buried in a grave.

In a way, the soul is like an automobile engine waiting to be used. If the ignition isn't turned on, it doesn't fulfill its purpose. And if it is used and isn't properly maintained, it will break down and seize. Like the car's engine, the soul requires proper maintenance. Proper maintenance of the soul occurs when we faithfully apply the guidance from our Higher Power that is designed for our spiritual development.

The process sounds simple, doesn't it? And it *is* simple if you know where to find the guidance and how it is given. Certainly, a giant hand does not dip down from the sky and drop divine guidelines into a particular house of worship. Information about how divine guidance is attained will be shared in a later chapter.

THINGS YOU CAN DO:

1. Accept the fact that there is only one race, the human race. Become familiar with the realities underlying the oneness of the human family. There are various books mentioned in this section and in the bibliography that can help you gain an understanding of these realities. There are many other sources you can turn to such as the World Wide Web, your local library, or a nearby university.

2. Remember that there is an invisible chain called breathing that links all living creatures together. You are connected in a very real sense with everyone else on the planet.

3. Take a walk and look at the diversity in the world of nature. Think about how boring life would be if everything and everyone were the same. Ponder this saying: "The diversity of the human family should be the cause of love and harmony as it is in music, where many different notes are blended together to make a perfect chord."[2]

4. Keep in mind that we are all at most fiftieth cousins, and if someone harms you, you are being harmed by a family member. Maybe this will help you to be more forgiving.

5. Gaze at the night sky and ponder the immensity and magnificence of a universe given with grace by an Invisible Hand. Think about your role in creation. Think about the following quotation: "This grand show is eternal. It is always sunrise somewhere: the dew is never all dry at once: a shower is forever falling, vapor is ever rising. Eternal sunrise, eternal sunset, eternal dawn and gloaming, on sea and continents and islands, each in its turn, as the round earth rolls."[3]

6. By making a commitment to find ways to break out of the trap, we are led to a spiritual awakening. Remember that no one can do it for you. Search and question.

STEP TWO *The Soul*

STEP ONE *Oneness*

6

The Nature of the Soul

During a lifelong search for meaning, I developed a philosophy through personal and group study, through meditation, and through interviews and dialogue with respected as well as little-known wise thinkers residing in different parts of the world. Along the way I gained insights that made me feel like a blind man who had just regained his sight. Such experiences inspired me to probe further.

My life was transformed when I discovered that I am not merely a body, nor for that matter a body that happens to have a soul. Like every other human being, I am a soul that happens to have a body. As a result of this new awareness, I found myself on a course I never knew existed. My inner eye opened, and I began to understand things I was incapable of grasping prior to my awakening. This awakening didn't come as a sudden burst of enlightenment but rather as a gradual growth of awareness, much like the unfoldment of a new day. But the skies were not always clear; there were storms that came in the form of doubts. Fortunately, with effort and persistence, they faded away.

I am not endowed with any special powers. All humans possess the capacity to see and know what I now see and know—and more. It is simply a matter of gaining a clearer view of reality and understanding our responsibility to develop our souls.

Psychiatrist M. Scott Peck stresses the importance of developing the soul as a means of healing our emotional wounds and gaining meaning in our lives. In his book *Further Along the Road Less Traveled,* he points out that a person can be "religious" and still be unaware of the need to develop his soul. Dr. Peck tells of a patient—a devout Christian woman married to a minister—who had been seeing him for a year and making no progress at all. Then one day she announced at the start of the session that while driving to Dr. Peck's office she realized that what's most important in life is the development of her soul. With that understanding the woman made considerable progress in therapy.[1]

A dedicated Christian, Dr. Peck adds that he suspects most Christians are not aware of the individual's responsibility to develop his or her soul. I would further add that most people fall into the same category: They haven't the faintest idea of what the soul is, let alone their responsibility for its development.

I have come to the conclusion that without understanding and developing our souls, we will never gain inner peace.

The soul comes into being at the point of conception. While it has a beginning, it has no end. Unlike the body, it is an intangible single spiritual entity—an unknown essence— that is not subject to the laws of composition and decomposition. It is indestructible. The soul is not inside the body, nor is it attached to it. In a sense, the soul is associated with the body much like a light that's focused on a mirror. You can't pull the light out of the mirror. Should the mirror fall and break, the light continues to shine.

The soul is a spiritual emanation of an organizing force some call the Universal Mind, the Absolute, Higher Power, or God. There is a connection between the human soul and this life-creating, life-sustaining, unknowable essence—a connection that can be likened to the relationship between the sun and its rays. When an individual ignores or rejects the soul, they ignore or reject their connection with God, Who is the source of all love and knowledge. When they choose not to acknowledge this source, they are forced to rely on the instincts and appetites that propel the animal, and they are prone to behave in what society condemns as "evil ways."* Although it may seem presumptuous on my part to try to describe something so ethereal as the structure of the individual human being's connection with the Creator, I am going to try, based on clues I have gained from the teachings of the Founders of the world's great religions.

Our connection with the Higher Power seems to take a circular route. The soul's journey in life starts out and ends up in the same place—in the spirit world of our Creator.

Dreaming is a sign of the soul's existence. When we sleep, we are closer to death than in any other human condition. While the soul doesn't possess ears, a nose, a tongue, legs, or eyes, in our dreams we are able nonetheless to converse, smell odors, run and touch others, meet people and see things we have never met or seen before, and travel to places we have

---

* Evil is not an active force. It is the absence of good, just as darkness is the absence of light and cold is the absence of heat. Just as the Sun is the source of all life in our solar system, so ultimately is there only one force in the universe, and that is God.

never been to before. Our dreams can have a profound impact on us, especially when we find ourselves for the first time in a place we have dreamed about, meeting people who were in our dreams and who change our lives.

An American couple revealed such an experience on national television. The wife, who wanted to have another child but couldn't produce one naturally, had a vivid dream of a light-skinned woman giving birth to a black-haired, olive-skinned boy. When she awoke she glanced at her calendar and clock and made note of the day and time: March 8, 2:59 AM.

Shortly after sharing the dream with her husband, the couple received a call from an adoption agency stating that it had found an infant boy for them. When the wife saw the baby, she gasped because it was the same child she had seen being born in her dream. "What day was the child born?" she asked. "March 8th," said the social worker. "And the time of birth?" asked the wife. The social worker checked the chart she was holding and said, "2:59 AM."

After explaining why she was asking the questions, the wife asked if she could see a picture of the biological mother. When the social worker drew the photo out of the file drawer and showed it to the couple, the wife exclaimed, "That's the woman in my dream." Though there is no scientific explanation for the wife's dream, the experience was real, springing from an aspect of our nature that many scientists reject or know very little about.

The soul is our true reality. Inherent in the soul are certain qualities that most of us admire and wish we could manifest at all times. Truthfulness, compassion, love, integrity, selflessness, humility, fair-mindedness, and courtesy are some of these qualities. All of them and more are latent within the soul, just as the color, the fragrance, and the vitality of a flower are latent within the seed. Every infant who comes into this world possesses latent virtues. This is what makes us potentially good.

It is the parents' responsibility to help their child discover, release, and develop those latent virtues. School teachers have that responsibility, too. Unfortunately, ignorance of these simple facts prevents many parents and teachers from carrying out their responsibilities. They possess an erroneous view of what it means to be human, believing that all men and women are fundamentally evil, born in "original sin." Imagine trying to drum divine virtues into children you believe to be basically bad. With that kind of attitude, parents often resort to verbal abuse and, at times, beatings to achieve their ends. Such harsh and twisted moral educational practices have long been used by parents and schools, and are still employed today in too many homes and schools. Trying to drum virtues into a person in this way is like trying to nail plastic branches onto a live tree trunk and hoping they will grow.

The divine virtues latent within the soul are like seeds. If they are to grow and fulfill their potential, they need to be properly and regularly nourished. When this occurs, the virtues become firmly established and grow more prominent in a person's life, like sturdy branches on a tree.

Ideally, the nourishment takes the form of a home environment that stimulates development of the virtues. While parents must teach their children about the nature of a human being, they must also impress upon them the importance of continually cultivating their virtues and must show them how it is done by example. Finding the time to give youngsters undivided attention, expressing unqualified love for them, holding their hands, or placing an arm around their shoulders while talking to them are all examples of positive nourishment. When a child exhibits an attribute like kindness or compassion, it should be enthusiastically acknowledged by the parent and teacher. A child usually values whatever makes a parent or teacher happy. Whenever punishment is necessary, always focus on the act that provokes the punishment and not the child. Before the punishment is carried out, children should understand why they are being punished so they don't repeat the unacceptable act. And when parents mistreat their children, they should always find time to apologize to them. Making an apology shows the parent's respect for the child and teaches the youngster respect by example.

In contrast, if we believe that human beings are purely animal in nature, we will expect animalistic behavior and see life as a jungle where might makes right and beating out the next guy is considered natural and desirable. We will see loving and compassionate people as fools and will think thoughtfulness, courtesy, and generosity are means to achieve selfish ends.

But the human being is far more than an animal, and being a soul makes each and every human being potentially divine. The soul possesses the powers of thought, comprehension, and imagination. Inner vision is another faculty of the soul. It is the source of all original and intuitive ideas. The difference between the brain and inner vision is that inner vision knows and the brain reasons.

Using their inner sight, many scientists see a meaningful idea unfold and know it is right. To prove it to their colleagues, they employ reasoning vehicles such as the scientific method and mathematics. Helen Keller, the incomparable blind and deaf poet and philosopher, had a keen inner sight. She often saw and felt things that most sighted people will never see or feel in their lifetime: "I sense the rush of ethereal rains . . . I possess the light which shall give me vision a thousand-fold when death sets me free."[2]

As you can see, the human being comes into existence with certain powers and attributes that must be discovered and developed. Among these powers are the yearnings to know, to love, and to be loved. To assure good health, these yearnings must be satisfied from birth through old age. If they are neglected, we can become emotionally crippled, physically ill, or worse. Infants are known to have died because of a lack of love. A poor student knows that if the yearning for knowledge can't be fulfilled in school, she'll seek fulfillment elsewhere, usually the street. Adults who stop learning or who are deprived of a loving relationship suffer from despair.

At the outset, nature assists us in satisfying these yearnings. The infant's need to know and to love and be loved is satisfied when he finds his mother's breast and suckles and is stroked by her. But these yearnings are to be used for an even greater purpose than creating healthy human relationships. The soul's impulses to know, to love, and to be loved should be used to strengthen our connection with God. Above all, the powers of knowing and loving are to be used to know and love our Creator. Through this relationship we become greater lovers of our fellow human beings and gain a greater understanding of reality.

Even those who reject the idea of a soul or have a different understanding of the soul employ its powers. For the soul, like a mirror, reflects what is put before it, and the human being determines what is put before it. If, on the one hand, the soul is trained only on the physical world, its powers will be used to carry out material desires. If, on the other hand, it is trained heavenward, its powers will be used to fulfill spiritual pursuits and develop virtues. A spiritually developing person will attain a penetrative sight and will have the capacity to see the reality of others and hear the inner voice of those who are troubled. Such a person is able to learn the truth because she hears more than words and senses the real meaning behind the words. All human beings have the capacity to develop this ability. It evolves from dedication to one's personal spiritual development. I became aware of this power myself through an unusual experience with one of my students.

Josh was a twenty-seven-year-old man who had just been released from the penitentiary and matriculated into a teacher's college program. The six-foot-seven, 250-pound young man wanted desperately to succeed in life, especially for the sake of his six-year-old son, who had been abandoned by his mother and cared for by his grandmother while Josh was in prison. The boy was now living with his father, a single parent who wanted to create a wholesome environment for his son and wanted desperately to provide him with a healthy role model.

Josh was doing so well in his program that I decided to arrange for him to do an internship. When I broke the good news to Josh, I was taken aback by Josh's reaction. "I'm not going," he shouted, turning mean and tight-lipped. At first I was angry, for I had gone out of my way to get Josh a choice internship, one that would draw him closer to realizing his career goal. But after collecting myself, I realized what Josh was really saying through his angry refusal: I am not going to take the internship because I feel comfortable in this college program. I can be myself. For the first time, I'm getting good grades. If I go someplace else, especially where someone is likely to ridicule or cross me, I might lose my temper and end up back in jail. And what would happen to my son?

I asked Josh to come to my office. Inside, the student sat ramrod straight, facing the man he had trusted, still sneering, his tightly clenched fists planted on his lap. Though I felt uneasy—after all, the giant of a man before me had been in jail for assault and battery—I had to find a way to penetrate Josh's armor. Fearful of saying the wrong thing, I resorted to prayer. It was the only thing I could do. I made a silent pact with God: "God, whatever passes from my lips is not from me, but from you." I looked into Josh's eyes and said, "If you don't take the internship, I'm going to kick your ass."

I was startled, not only by what I had uttered, but also by Josh's reaction. The young man began crying, sobbing uncontrollably. I realized that what Josh had heard was not what passed from my lips but what streamed from my heart. What Josh heard was, "I love you," and Josh had not heard that for a very long time. To him, I had become the father he never had, and he decided to obey his father.

Though the soul is meant to be developed, humans are endowed with a free will. We are free to reject the notion of a soul and ignore its development if we wish. However, this freedom to choose, combined with our powers of thought, memory, speech, intuition, imagination—all powers of the soul—means that we have the capacity to do evil things. A gorilla can do a lot of physical destruction, but he can't do what Hitler or Stalin did. It was Thomas Aquinas, the thirteenth-century Christian theologian, who said, "One human being can do more evil than all the other species of creatures put together."[3] Though the physical aspect of human nature is the repository and generator of our senses, it has another important function: The physical aspect demonstrates and carries out what the spiritual aspect initiates. For example, without our body, a strong desire to help an elderly person cross the street would remain nothing more than a good intention. So a healthy body is not only necessary to produce a healthy child; it is essential to carrying out our spiritual impulses.

In reality, both aspects of human nature are dependent on each other to carry out their ordained purpose, which is to create a loving and caring human being who, in turn, becomes a positive influence in his or her community. To live a good life, I believe, is to continually manifest the attributes of the soul in all of your interactions. This requires that both aspects of our nature must be regularly cared for. When this balance is maintained, each aspect becomes clearly defined: The spiritual aspect becomes more assertive, and the physical aspect becomes more submissive— then and only then are they performing their ideal functions. As the soul develops and matures, it not only initiates positive ideas but prompts the physical aspect to take virtuous action. In other words, the result of such a cooperative union is a highly developed conscience, which acts as a catalyst for doing good deeds.

It is interesting that science has discovered a built-in reward system within the human organism. When a person does a good deed, the brain releases endorphins, creating a sense of well–being, or a natural high. In a way, the natural high is the soul's way of showing its gratitude to the body for carrying out its command. I have learned that good deeds that obviously cheer the hearts of the recipients generate supercharged natural highs in the one who performs a good deed.

It seems that human beings are meant to have these natural highs, so it is understandable why some desperate people reach for potions that generate artificial highs, which in the long run are destructive to the body. I have observed that those who are not involved in doing good deeds and successfully resist taking drugs or alcohol tend to be sour in disposition, negative, self-righteous, judgmental, bitter, and perpetually fearful. Why are human beings supposed to have natural highs? Because they are meant to do good deeds. Within each one of us is a limitless reservoir of potential goodness. Dr. Elisabeth Kübler-Ross, in her book *Working It Through,* reminds us of this aspect of reality:

There is within each one of us a potential for goodness beyond our imagination; for giving which seeks no reward; for listening without judgment; for loving unconditionally. It is our goal to reach that potential. We can approach it, in ways large and small every minute of every day, if we try. When we have found that path, we have built our own "home of peace" inside of ourselves.[4]

Obviously, the world would be a happier and safer place if the majority of people were to set their minds to discovering, developing, and using their latent goodness to do good deeds. Ideally, we should be on a perpetual natural high. This can be described as a feeling of inner security, inner strength, the feeling of possessing an incorruptible spirit, having a sense of one's destiny and knowing how to reach it, deriving pleasure from helping others, and being in a joyous mood. Unfortunately, most do not know that this is their birthright. Certainly the religious extremists don't. While they acknowledge the existence of the soul, they look upon the body as the soul's natural enemy. They consider the body sinful and the soul divine, believing that there should be no association between them. As a result, they often resort to physical or mental flagellation—or both—in order to drive the "devil"* out of themselves. This fanatical mind-set, fueled by superstition and ignorance, has led many sincere seekers of truth to lose their respect for religion and to stop trying to understand the purpose of the soul.

---

* In reality there is no superhuman entity called the Devil. The term is a metaphor for the human ego that rejects God's guidelines for living. The natural consequence of such rejection is to rely purely on one's physical instincts. Obsessed with survival, such a person will resort to any means to assure his safety and is liable to succumb to greed, anger, hatred, violence, and slander, reflecting the qualities we normally attribute to the mythical "Devil." A collection of such spiritually unawakened souls can create a "hellish" atmosphere in a community.

Those who don't give up eventually gain a basic under-standing of their spiritual nature and realize that they are a soul with a body, not a body with a soul. They learn that in an ideal state, the body, which eventually disintegrates, is the servant of the soul, which remains intact eternally. Cer-tainly Teilhard de Chardin understood, for he believed that "We are not human beings having a spiritual experience, we are spiritual beings having a human experience."[5]

A friend named Julio also understood this concept. While most of those who knew him didn't understand, they were drawn to him and wanted to be in his presence because he brought out the best in them. In his fortieth year he left his native Puerto Rico, settling in a Latino neighborhood of a large industrial American city. He operated a shoe-repair shop in the same place for nearly thirty-five years, living in the same two-room flat during that time.

Though Julio never married, he claimed to have many children. All of the boys and girls of the neighborhood, he felt, were his. Julio was considered the community's grand-father, and he relished the role. It wasn't only the cookies and fruit he would hand out to the children who dropped by after school that impressed them and their parents. When he talked to the children, he always built up their self-es-teem and encouraged them to pursue a college education. For those who couldn't afford to go to college, he offered to help finance their way.

Julio helped more than seventy-five youngsters fulfill their educational dreams. Those graduates who wanted to pay him back were told to give the money to a special fund he had set up to help others achieve what they had achieved. Often he would leave a bag of groceries at the door of a family he knew was unemployed. He visited the elderly regularly, especially those who lived alone. If they didn't know how to play chess, he would teach them. In time the elderly competed in their own annual neighborhood chess tournament.

Julio died on his seventy-fifth birthday in his bed at home. His funeral was an indication of the impact he had had on the community. More than two thousand people, including known gangsters and drug dealers, came to the church to pay their respects. Some even flew in from California and Texas.

To the people of the neighborhood, Julio's life was their description of goodness. They knew he was special in a positive sense, but they didn't know what made him special, what made him kind, generous, compassionate, and loving. Some viewed him as a real Christian, while others felt that he had to be an angel sent from God.

But Julio would have been the first to resist being called special, because he was aware of his shortcomings. What distinguished him from others was his awareness of his spiritual reality. He knew he was a soul. He worked at developing his soul, and as a result he continually grew kinder, more compassionate, more loving—developing qualities that everyone has the potential to develop. The fact that Julio knew these things made him wise.

7

Spiritual Development

Physical conditions such as heat and cold and suffering don't concern the soul—they only concern the body. Therefore pain and anguish don't affect the essence and basic characteristics of the soul. Yet behaviors such as lying and backbiting, though they cannot alter the nature of the soul, do impede its ability to grow and manifest its inherent qualities, much like dross and dirt prevent a mirror from fulfilling its purpose. Removal of the dross and dirt depends on the efforts to develop the soul's latent qualities. By becoming consistently truthful, loving, courteous, humble, kind, and generous, the soul eventually dominates the physical nature, and the human being becomes what our Creator meant for us to be—a saint.[1]

Just as it is essential to keep cleaning a mirror periodically to keep the dross from collecting on its surface, it is essential to continue developing the soul's powers and qualities if we wish to grow spiritually. Spiritual development is therefore a lifelong process.

When we ignore the needs of the soul, we become captives of the physical aspect of our nature and cannot reflect our true spiritual nature. In doing so, we stray from the prescribed course that all human beings are meant to take, believing that when the body experiences total breakdown, life ends.

The major reason for straying from this course is lack of awareness or a distorted view resulting from man-made dogma and theology or materialistic philosophies. The journey of life begins at the point of conception. In the mother's womb, the embryo develops limbs and organs that it will need when it emerges from the womb. Obviously the child isn't meant to remain in its mother's womb. Arms, legs, eyes, and ears develop in the womb, but they are not used there. In fact, the fetus doesn't exercise free will; it is wholly dependent on its mother, who shares her blood chemistry with it through the umbilical cord. Indeed, there is even evidence that a woman's moods when she is pregnant greatly influence her child's attitudes and behavior in ways that will affect the child when he becomes an adult.

In this plane of existence, however, the child in infancy begins to exercise its free will, which becomes more pronounced around two years of age. During adolescence children often flaunt their free will as a signal to their parents that they are about to cross the threshold leading to adulthood.

In adolescence and adulthood, a human being can freely choose to ignore his or her soul, relying on physical instincts to deal with life's myriad problems and needs. However, to choose that path is to turn off the prescribed course and head for disaster, toward the spiritual condition that grips much of the world today. To stay on course requires constant involvement in a process of spiritual development. (The process will be discussed in a later chapter.) In reality, the child passes from the confined womb of the mother into the womb of this world, equipped to use and strengthen what was developed inside the mother. For example, the infant's eyes cannot see inside the mother's womb, but after birth occurs, the light of this world brings vision to the child's eyes. Just as the embryo develops body parts that are to be used in this plane of existence, the human being is supposed to be developing his or her soul in this world for use in the life hereafter.

While the gestation period of an embryo is about nine months, the human being's average life span in this world, barring accidental death, is approximately seventy-five years. Unlike the embryo that develops limbs and organs that are useless before birth, a human being develops virtues that are to be tried and tested again and again before they are needed in the next life. This process of trying and testing is no mere exercise regimen. Its purpose is to unite the human family and establish world peace. This ideal condition can only be achieved if the great majority of human beings are seriously involved in developing the latent divine qualities within their souls. In this part of the journey—the here-and-now—life is meant to be a struggle. To those who repudiate the essence of their own being and neglect their spiritual development, the struggle takes the form of competition or a sense of powerlessness. They measure their success in terms of how many competitors they vanquish; the more victories they amass, the more successful they think they are. When the majority of a population engages in that kind of struggle, a dog-eat-dog spirit prevails, creating the kind of society that prevails in much of the world today. While struggle is a natural characteristic of life's journey in this plane of existence, it is not meant to be carried out on a battlefield or the marketplace.

The late social and religious thinker Horace Holley wrote in his book *Religion for Mankind,* "The energy of personal struggle has been misunderstood and misapplied. The real purpose of that endowment is to equip the individual human being with capacity, not to overcome his fellow, but to transcend himself."[2]

Ideally, the human struggle is to be directed at overcoming the pull of the physical aspect of our nature and replacing it with a more transcendent balance between the spiritual and physical. If the soul is continually nourished, it takes its rightful place in its association with the body. This is not an easy task when the nourishing must take place in an unsympathetic climate, in a community obsessed with competition. There are the materialistic temptations, the countless tests, the personal physical drives that are continually stimulated by the media's programming and advertising. All of these competing interests reflect the profound absence of a spiritual dimension in our lives, leaving us unbalanced and crippled, our society deranged.

As our spiritual awareness grows, we realize that the soul's development is never-ending. Life becomes an ongoing workshop in which continual strengthening of character takes place. The struggle does not end until we take our last breath.

The next phase of life's journey begins at death, when we leave the womb of this world. At that point the association between body and soul ends; the body returns to the earth— its atoms are dispersed into the soil and atmosphere, becoming part of other living creatures on the planet.

When the association between body and soul ends, the soul soars into the next phase of its destiny, into the spiritual worlds of God. But this is not a tangible place with pearly gates and grinning angels floating about in white gowns, strumming golden harps. Nor is there a fiery place called "hell."* In fact, we do not know what the spiritual world will be like in the life hereafter, for the human being in this plane of existence, like the embryo in the mother's womb, cannot conceive of what comes next. However, the divine prophets have given us some clues. A search through the sacred texts of the world's great religions reveals that once we pass into the next life, we are freed from the tensions, fears, prejudices, and anxieties of this world, yet we retain whatever knowledge, wisdom, and insights we attained on the earthly plane. We become aware of whatever was hidden from us in this life and comprehend all things with the eye of the soul, our inner eye.

Fortunately, those souls who have neglected their spiritual development in this world can still progress in the life hereafter through the bounty of God, through the sincere prayers of other souls, and through good works performed in their name. Although I have described the worlds of the mother's womb, the here and now, and life after death as if they were three separate worlds, and although they represent three distinct stages of development in life's journey, they are actually one and the same. All of creation is a single entity. This will become apparent when we pass into the next plane of existence.

Believing that the here and now is a world separate from the life hereafter is like believing that the mother's womb is a

---

* Heaven and hell are conditions—psychological and spiritual states of being—not literal places. Heaven is the natural consequence of spiritual progress, while hell represents the results of failure to progress spiritually.

separate world from the here and now. Though the embryo is unaware of this plane of existence, it is already in this plane of existence because the woman who is carrying it is here. This aspect of reality becomes apparent as children mature. As adults they eventually realize that when they were inside their mother's womb, all that prevented them from experiencing the outside world was a thin membrane. The child in the womb is like the chick within the egg, unaware of this world until it breaks through its fragile shell. The same is true for us as we try to grasp the relationship of the life hereafter to this plane of existence. Our heavy reliance on our physical senses veils us from understanding and accepting this aspect of reality.

However, it seems that the more spiritually centered we become, the less we fear death. At times—perhaps during moments of deep reflection—our inner vision penetrates the veils between this life and the next, and what we know about the spiritual world is reinforced. The late writer and social activist Brenda Ueland was one of those insightful persons: "You know much brighter souls than I, Blake, Swedenborg, and Jesus, great souls more pervious to the Invisible than I am, say that when we die we are not dead. I cannot help but believe that. It is a certitude. I cannot go away from the notion. Death is unbearably tragic and grievous because it is a kind of farewell. But it is not forever. Those who are Yonder, in a queer way—I have discovered this myself—are more pulsant than ever. They are more befriending, more strengthening, more helpful."[3]

The spiritually developing human being senses from time to time a natural pull toward the next world. This has nothing to do with wanting to commit suicide. It is, rather, a yearning to improve one's condition in this world. The person who feels this way senses that something could be gained from the next life that would be beneficial in this one.

Some psychiatrists believe there are practical benefits to leading a vibrant spiritual life that includes a belief in life after death. The famed Swiss psychiatrist Carl Jung stated in his essay *The Stages of Life* that a belief in life after death makes the here and now more meaningful and healthy: "I have observed that a life directed to an aim is in general better, richer, and healthier than an aimless one. . . . As a doctor, I am convinced that it is hygienic to discover in death a goal towards which one can strive, and that shrinking away from it is something unhealthy and abnormal which robs the second half of life of its purpose."[4]

Some scientists are trying to probe into the next life. To do this, Dr. R. A. Moody, the author of *Life After Life*, has interviewed hundreds of women and men who have had clinical death or near-death experiences. Based on these discussions, he has discovered sufficient parallels to enable him to draw up a profile of the life hereafter. While not everyone has had the same experience, the great majority share some similar characteristics. The similarities are so striking that Dr. Moody has been inspired to continue his probing.

One of Moody's supporters, Dr. Elisabeth Kübler-Ross, one of the leading authorities in the field of death counseling, suggests that those who truly understand the death process aren't fearful of the transition to another existence: "Death is the final stage of growth in this life. There is no total death. Only the body dies. The self [the soul] or spirit, or whatever you may wish to label it, is eternal. You may interpret this in any way that makes you comfortable. . . . Death, in this context, may be viewed as the curtain between the existence we are conscious of and the one that is hidden from us until we raise that curtain."[5]

While Elisabeth Kübler-Ross and R. A. Moody have heard hundreds of women and men relate their near-death experiences, others like myself have also met people who have been suddenly whisked into the next life—for a brief sojourn—and have come back to share their experience. Usually those who have had such experiences hesitate to share them with others, because most people don't believe them. And some, like Sally, a successful financial planner, are ridiculed and mocked. Her closest friends thought that perhaps she had converted to some esoteric religious sect or was taking LSD. Some even felt that she was under the spell of some Svengali.

One night some of us sat spellbound to hear her story. "My ulcerative colitis was literally killing me. It was either have the operation—or die. Well, I had the operation and died anyway." Sally's laughter was infectious, for we started laughing as well. About two minutes later when we had all calmed down, Sally continued speaking:

I still don't know the reason why my heart stopped pumping on the operating table. It took, I am told, twenty minutes to bring me back. That's right! I was somewhere that I had no plans to visit, or had any idea existed. But I knew that I existed there, even though I had no arms or legs or eyes or ears. Yet I could see and hear, but more than that. I could tell what the doctors and nurses were thinking and feeling. And I seemed to be hovering over them.

They were working feverishly on my body. Obviously frustrated, the head surgeon used the foulest language. The poor man was trying so hard to save me. I remember trying to assure the medical team that I was okay, and not to worry, that the slab of meat on the operating table wasn't me. Then suddenly there was a banging sensation, and I was sucked into what seemed like a dark tunnel. As I moved through it I was exposed to flashbacks of many experiences I had had, and most of what I saw were things that I was ashamed of, stuff that at the time I had done in order to beat out a business competitor or vanquish an enemy. For the first time I experienced shame, but more importantly I gained an understanding of what kind of achievements in this life have the greatest value. It isn't writing books, building bridges, traveling to the moon, amassing a fortune, or winning a world soccer championship.

What matters most are the simple acts of kindness, compassion, and love we manifest toward our fellow human beings. When I left the tunnel and was exposed to the most brilliant light I had ever seen, I felt a freedom I had never experienced before. Every fear, every worry, every conflict was gone. It was as if a mighty weight had been lifted from my back. All I felt was joy, unadulterated joy, complete freedom. For the first time in my life I knew what it was like to be free. Oh, I wanted to go farther, wherever that light would direct me, I was ready to go.

Then I saw people whom I had known—and that had died. I saw my father, and his mother. They were happy to see me. Others showed up. It seemed like a reunion was about to take place, when that figure appeared. The look on his face. I will never forget it. So calm. His smile reflected a love for me that I couldn't resist. Nothing sexual, mind you. It was pure love, the kind I had never experienced before. I knew that I would do whatever he asked me to do. There was absolutely no question about that.

When he pointed to the opposite direction, away from those who had gathered to greet me, I knew I had to go back. And they knew it, too. Somehow, I felt there were things that had to be done back here, that involved me. I didn't know at the time what it was going to be, but I was certain I had things to do, important things. As soon as I turned back, everything went blank.

When I opened my eyes I found myself in a private hospital room, with two tubes stuck in my arm. Strange, but I wasn't happy—for the lack of a better term—to be alive. I missed that feeling I had experienced in that special place that really wasn't a place, because there was nothing tangible there, yet I know it existed. Though I wasn't happy being back, I was resigned to being back, for I knew that that was what God wanted for me. In coming to that realization, I acknowledged God, something that I had neglected to do seriously for nearly ten years of climbing the ladder of success.

As I lay in that bed, I knew that I would never be the same person who had been wheeled into the operating room to get rid of the pain that was thwarting my goal of making ten million dollars by the time I reached forty. When the doctor appeared—the one who had used the foul language—he pulled up a chair and said, "You're going to be all right. You should be up and around in two days."

Then he put his hand on mine and added in a somber voice, "You know, we almost lost you."

"I know," I said.

Though the doctor seemed surprised at my response, he never inquired as to how I knew, he simply patted my hand several times and assured me, "you will be as good as new."

Sally smiled, and said, "He didn't realize how right he was."

THINGS YOU CAN DO:

1. When pondering your true reality, remember that you are a soul with a body, not a body with a soul.

2. Tap the powers of your soul in dealing with life's challenges through intuition, creativity, and comprehension.

3. Discover and develop the latent virtues within your soul (for example, love, compassion, truthfulness).

4. Know that you are inherently good and that everyone around you is inherently good. Don't dwell on the negative qualities in yourself or others.

5. Try to do something creative every day. Creativity enables us to use our inner sight and puts us in a positive frame of mind.

6. By thinking about life after death daily, passing on will be a natural progression and not a horror.

7. Ponder the three phases of life's journey: the mother's womb, the here and now, and the life hereafter. Take to heart what we are supposed to do in the here and now, which is a preparation for life in the next world.

STEP THREE *Religion & the Divine Educators*

STEP TWO *The Soul*

STEP ONE *Oneness*

8

The Rise and Fall of Religion

One of religion's greatest contributions to human development is its announcement and continual reaffirmation of the reality of the human soul. Throughout the ages, religion has kept humanity's spiritual embers alive, continually reminding us that there is a spiritual dimension to our makeup. Some exceptional individuals discovered and wholeheartedly applied the divine guidance on how to nourish the soul and developed into spiritual beacons—individuals such as St. Francis of Assisi, Florence Nightingale, Martin Buber, Helen Keller, Mohandas Gandhi, and Albert Schweitzer.

Connecting with such guidance wasn't easy because it was often obscured by layers of man-made theology that reflected a distorted view of human nature and the purpose of life. One can surmise that genuine prayers helped, as did a persistent spirit and an open mind.

Tragically, however, the great majority of religious adherents have not connected with the divine guidance that, for example, Mother Teresa plugged into. They became stuck in the mire of dogma and ritual. Sadly, most are either unaware that they are stuck or are afraid to admit it. They forge ahead, enthusiastically promoting religious interpretations that lack the power to nourish the soul. As a consequence, their activities fail to solve the real problems that face the world today.

Practices such as circumcision and baptism won't hasten the development of the soul, nor will confession to priests. Not even the communion ceremony will help. Religious rituals will not curtail the potential for humans to behave in a beastly manner. Millions of baptized American, English, German, and Italian soldiers—virtually all of them Christians—were shooting at each other during World War II with chaplains on both sides beseeching God to keep their men injury-free and, of course, victorious. Iraqi and Iranian Muslims, clutching Korans, spent eight years killing each other on the battlefield. So much energy has gone into praying to statues, kissing priests' hands, and adoring church trappings that traditional organized religion, for the most part, no longer reflects the spirit of God.

After a cursory survey of world conditions, most observers would conclude that religion has made a mess of things. But there is another way to look at it. Actually, *people* have made a mess of religion.

Having created human beings with a soul, our merciful and all-loving Creator has never left us without spiritual guidance and never will. God has chosen religion as the primary channel for delivering His guidance to humanity. The trouble is that through the centuries the divine channel has become clogged, for the most part, with misguided man-made interpretations of the Word of God and religious rites that are devoid of spirituality.

The late Christian theologian Nels Ferré was aware of this condition. He described it in a book titled *The Sun and the Umbrella*. In his expanded parable, he likens God to the sun and today's church to an umbrella. Because man holds onto the umbrella or the church, he is shielded from the sun and from God. What the parishioner thinks is God's guidance is really man-made dictums based on church-created dogma.[1]

Though it is a difficult concept to accept, especially for members of religious hierarchies, traditional organized religion is, for the most part, a far cry from what religion was meant to be. The evidence is clear. No special investigations are necessary. Any honest cleric would agree that the political jockeying for power within many religious institutions has no place in religion and that the prejudices of various congregations that dictate the social attitudes of certain religious organizations are equally out of place. Certainly, there is no place for the growing moral debauchery that seems increasingly evident among so many clerics and parishioners. Any discerning person can see that if traditional organized religion were doing what it is supposed to do—serving as a force for unity—the world wouldn't be in the awful condition it's in. It simply lacks the vision and dynamism to set the right course for a humanity that is groaning for a way out of the trap.

One of the reasons for the grave condition of traditional organized religion is its disunity. This disunity is fueled by ancient prejudices and animosities and perpetuated because of our unawareness or rejection of an important aspect of reality: the fundamental oneness of religion.

Just as a distorted understanding of human nature has prevented us from realizing our spiritual potential, a distorted understanding of religion has kept us from fulfilling our ultimate purpose—which is to be the cause of unity among the believers of God. The very word *religion* stems from the Latin word *religio,* which means "to bind together."

Instead of binding together the children of God, religion has had the opposite effect. Within Christianity alone, according to the *World Christian Encyclopedia,* there are at least twenty thousand sects.

What went wrong? The religious leadership, for the most part, has been unable and unwilling to recognize the fundamental oneness of religion. This doesn't mean that Moses and Jesus Christ weren't who they claimed to be. But the theologians' "keyhole" interpretations of the divine prophets' nature and role in advancing the cause of religion has given rise to conflicting theories that have become hardened doctrine.

It stands to reason that the major divine prophets of God didn't come to compete with one another. Jesus did not oppose Moses or revoke the Ten Commandments. On the contrary, he declared that he came not to destroy the law, and added *"Had ye believed in Moses, ye would have believed in me."* (John 5:44) Nor did Muḥammad try to devalue his predecessors' contributions. Actually, they came to complement one another, to further the one religion of God, not to divide it into rival factions that would war against one another.

Ideally, the one religion of God is meant to evolve through divine revelation and serve the family of man by providing continual guidance on how to develop the spiritual and physical aspects of human nature and how to create a healthy, unified community. One of the greatest historians of the twentieth century, Arnold Toynbee, recognized the essential oneness of religion: "At first sight, Buddhism, Christianity and Islam and Judaism may appear to be very different from each other. But when you look beneath the surface, you will find that all of them are addressing themselves primarily to the individual human psyche or soul; they are trying to persuade it to overcome its own self-centeredness and they are offering it the means for achieving this. They all find the same remedy. They all teach that egocentricity can be conquered by love."[2]

Religion can be likened to a school, with humanity as the student body and God as the principal. God creates the curriculum and selects the teachers. Spiritual development and social awareness are taught in every grade. The teachings in each grade build upon those of the previous teacher, taking into account the students' level of maturity. You don't teach calculus to four- or five-year-olds, even though they have the potential to master it someday. A foundation in mathematics must be built first. Wouldn't a wise and compassionate principal educate that way?

The divine educators such as Moses or Jesus are teachers in God's school. Though their names are different and they came at different times and different places, their mission is the same: to educate humanity so that it might develop to its fullest potential and to prepare to move to the next grade. In doing so, each divine educator reviews what his predecessors have taught. This is important, because much of what was taught in the past has become distorted. The light that each divine educator shines on the past cuts through the dust of dogma and theology, exposing the true identity and purpose of the divine educators who came before, thereby strength-

ening the foundation of the religion of God. He establishes
a new set of laws, some of which are identical to those taught
by previous divine teachers and some updated. He inspires
in his followers a renewed love for God, urges them to develop spiritually, provides guidance for creating a just and
spiritual society, and promises that others like him will come
in the future, continuing the divine teaching. This is a never-
ending process.

But most of us aren't aware of this aspect of reality, just as
the people of the past weren't aware that the world was round.
Yet this process continues, as it always has and always will. It
is a fundamental law of life.

As a species, humanity has ignored this spiritual truth time
after time, following the example of many misguided religious leaders. Instead of advancing to the next spiritual grade,
we have either fallen fanatically in love with the divine teacher
our forefathers revered, become indifferent toward him, or
rejected him as irrelevant. God is, among other things, practical. To direct Moses to inspire his followers to establish a
world government would have been a wasted effort, for it
was an idea the ancient Hebrews were incapable of grasping.
In time, as humanity matured, the establishment of a world
government would be a part of the teachings of a future divine educator.

Consider the state of the world in Jesus's day. How did
people perceive reality at that time? For most, their hamlet
or town was the center of the universe. Among the Roman
elite, the world was thought to consist of their empire, plus a
little more. Had someone told the people living two thousand years ago that one day there would be airplanes, televi-

sions, and human beings walking on the moon, that person would have been branded a lunatic. Although more and more of us recognize that nations will eventually have to unite and create one country on our planet, the people in Jesus's time weren't able to conceive of such a possibility. At the time, the planet was largely uncharted. Natural barriers—mighty mountain ranges, oceans, and seas—kept people apart. The people in North America weren't aware of the people in Burma, and the Burmese weren't aware of the North Americans. Hundreds of other tribes knew nothing of one another's existence. It would have been futile to call for the establishment of a world government; humanity wasn't ready for it. But one day it would be, and in that day, a divine educator would not only call for its development, but would also reveal a divine plan to implement it.

Makes sense doesn't it? Some of us might agree, but are skeptical, or are still emotionally attached to the established views of how God intervenes in humanity's development. Others among us might have difficulty accepting the evolutionary process of religion because it is too simple.

We may have turned "our own" divine educator into someone spiritually unique and superior to all the other divine educators, making it difficult for us to accept the others. But other divine educators have appeared and released new divine truth into the world. Sometimes elaborate attempts have been made to refute it. Even military campaigns have been organized to squelch what was condemned as the machinations of the devil. Throughout the ages God has sent divine educators to enlighten humankind, to guide us back to the spiritual path from which we tend to stray. And no earthly force, however powerful, has ever been able to prevent these divine educators from carrying out their missions. While we are aware of some of them, such as Moses, Buddha, Jesus, Zoroaster, and Muḥammad, there have been others in the distant past whose names we will never know.

The divine educators are unique in the grand phenomenon of life. They represent a special level of creation. None of history's great philosophers and statesmen can compare with them, not even such greats as Aristotle, Plato, Tolstoy, Tagore, or Gandhi. Nor are they to be compared with great religious leaders such as Martin Luther, the Dalai Lama, Mary Baker Eddy, or Joseph Smith. The divine educators are not simply humans with outstanding spiritual capacities. They are links between the Higher Power and humanity, divinely chosen channels transmitting divine direction for a particular age. In a sense, to know them is to know God, though they are not the same as God. They are, however, the closest we can get to God, for God is an unknowable essence. None of us, no matter how holy or perceptive we may be, can know God directly. Whatever picture of God we may imagine, whether male or female, it is an illusion, for no creation can know the mind of its creator. Although divine educators are seen by many, and historians may have written about them, we are essentially unable to grasp their true makeup.

The divine educator is a special being and because of that we are incapable of comprehending his nature. There are various levels of being in creation, and there might well be some that we know little about. Though these levels of life have certain things in common, there are fundamental differences. Furthermore, the lower levels simply cannot appreci-

ate the world of the higher levels. Can a lily understand a
bird? Can a dog truly understand a human being? Can we
really know the nature of a divine educator? No. But we can
feel the impact of the divine educators, whether we accept
their teachings or not. They do things no one else can do.
Because of them, great masses of people change their attitudes and behavior and grow spiritually. Their presence and
the knowledge and spiritual energy they release into the world
has given rise to great civilizations and changes in all phases
of life. It isn't a matter of accident or coincidence. The He-
brew, Christian, Muslim, Hindu, and Buddhist civilizations
didn't come into being through some magical formula concocted by anonymous figures in history.

There is no special physical characteristic that makes the
divine educator stand out. Outwardly, they are human, and
this is a frequent stumbling block for those who expect a
different kind of creature as God's earthly voice. They re-
semble us, and they are even susceptible to bodily imperfections. For instance, Moses is believed to have been a stut-
terer. Unlike us, however, the divine educator has completely
surrendered his will, manifesting only God's will. They do
not make choices based on their personal desires. Doing God's
will is their only reason for living, even though it means enduring constant hardship and often martyrdom.

The role of the divine educator is absolutely essential to our
relationship with God. Without him we would be guided by
nothing but fantasy. We would be like a crew on a captainless
ship, lost in a storm-tossed sea. To describe how God commu-
nicates with humanity through the divine educator, a metaphor is necessary. Think of God as the sun and the divine

educator as a mirror tilted toward the sun. When we look into the mirror, we can see the light of the sun. If we are close enough to the mirror, we can feel the sun's heat. Just as the mirror reflects the sun, the divine educator reflects the attributes of God. In that sense, when we turn to the divine educator, we are turning to God.

Historically, many people have had difficulty understanding the divine educators' relationship with God, yet they have been deeply touched by them. Logic and analysis usually had nothing to do with their decision to accept them. It was a matter of the heart. Often their followers' love for the divine educator grew so intense that the people became distracted and failed to grasp the teachings that were being offered to them. Their culture affected the way they perceived and followed the divine educator. St. Paul was aware of these cultural differences, so he adapted the story of Christ to the culture of whatever people he was teaching. To the Greeks, he emphasized one thing and to others he emphasized another. This may be one reason why there is such disparity in the way Christianity is practiced today.

There are two sides to the divine educator. His human side is distinctive because he is a unique individual. Like every human being, he has a childhood and playmates. He has favorite foods, experiences joy and sorrow, laughs and cries. He feels pain when lashed with a whip and bleeds when he is cut. He knows, too, the smells of the stable and the street. He is not what some religious artists have depicted—antiseptic, with his head constantly tilted skyward. Jesus was a carpenter, and among his friends were fishermen and prostitutes. Moses killed a man, and Muḥammad was an illiterate camel driver. Some of the divine educators married and had children.

Though each divine educator was a unique individual, there is no fundamental distinction between them from a spiritual point of view. They are all the repositories of the Holy Spirit. To better understand the two sides of the divine educator, think of him as a lighted lamp. The lamp represents his human form; the light, the holy spirit. Essentially the light is the same regardless of the lamp from which it radiates.

The divine educator not only sheds light on the present and future, caring for our spiritual and social needs, but also casts a bright, steady light on the past. This is necessary for us to appreciate his direction for the present and future; without it, our deeply entrenched, misguided notions and prejudices would keep us from understanding his message. He clarifies the identity and true purpose of his predecessors, exposing the dogma that prevents us from recognizing that information. Jesus, for example, said that if the people to whom he came had really known Moses, they would have known him.

Even those who sincerely accept the divine educator can unwittingly betray his purpose. For instance, if someone becomes so enamored of the lamp that he embraces it with such vigor that he blocks out the light, fanaticism follows. Though the essence of the divine educators' spiritual side is the same, there are quantitative differences between their revelations. Because the people of the past were not ready for the teachings of a later time, less illumination could be shed. But as humanity has advanced, more and more light has been cast.

Today our planet beckons for God's light. Mercifully, our appeal has already been heeded. Practically every spot on Earth is now illumined to a degree. Unfortunately, most people aren't yet aware of that fact, just as the great majority of people living about two thousand years ago were unaware of the spiritual light of Christ. It took centuries for large numbers of people to recognize that light.

9

A Crying Need for a Divine Educator

The divine educators and the educators in our schools—including the most accomplished ones—have little in common. For example, none of the divine educators ever earned a bachelor's degree or even an honorary doctoral degree, let alone a PhD.

In fact, while they dispensed knowledge and shared wisdom, the divine educators were never involved in scholarly pursuits. Lao-Tze said, "Wise men are never scholars and scholars are never wise men."[1] Scholars tend to be more narrowly focused, trying to uncover an aspect of reality through purely rational means, concentrating on various forms of minutia, while a wise person sheds light on reality based on her or his intuition, which is prompted by what the inner vision sees and knows is true. The wise person is a universal thinker who sees the connection in all things. It is interesting that the Lakota description of a wise person is someone who knows in her or his heart that all human beings are related to one another, that, in fact, all aspects of life are interrelated.

The divine educators are not only wise, they are also the revealers of God's Word for a particular age. They shed light on the right path, which we are supposed to find and follow during our life's journey. Perhaps the only thing divine educators have in common with regular school teachers is their mandate to educate. The source and substance of what divine educators and school teachers offer is fundamentally different. The divine educators' source is God. Functioning as a clear channel for divine directives, they do not pick and choose what aspects of their directives should be shared with humanity and in what order. Passing from their lips, in its purest form, is what God wishes for all of us to know, internalize, and put into practice.

The knowledge that the divine educator transmits is far more important to our well-being than the reading skills we acquired in elementary school or the principles of calculus we may have learned in college. It has to do with human beings gaining an understanding of their purpose in life and learning how to attain that highly prized goal. No present-day university, however great, provides this kind of knowledge.

As they learn and put into practice the divine educator's message, human beings will cease to use their reading and mathematical skills to design and carry out ethnic cleansing campaigns or to pursue business ventures that fleece clients. They will no longer engage in social practices that demean other human beings. They will instead use their acquired school learning to lift the spirit of their fellow human beings, to unify the human family, and to create a world civilization based on love and justice. In other words, the divine teachings will prompt human beings to do good deeds.

The teachings and spiritual standards revealed by the divine educators are the basis of the most cherished codes of morality from which ethical values emerge. Though humanity's moral fiber has weakened considerably of late, conditions would surely be far worse had Moses not revealed the Ten Commandments, had Jesus not given the Sermon on the Mount, had Buddha not revealed the Tenfold Course, or had Muḥammad not revealed the Koran. Unlike the instruction of a school teacher, which is directed primarily at the mind, the teachings of a divine educator penetrate the hearts and minds of people and motivate them to change their ways for the betterment of themselves and society. A dramatic example of this power can be seen in the acceptance of Muḥammad's teachings by barbarous Arabian tribes. The practice of burying infant girls alive ceased; the drinking of alcohol ended; women's rights were elevated; warring tribes were united; and a great civilization was born that vigorously promoted education, made significant scientific breakthroughs, and established universities, including the first one in Europe (in Córdoba, Spain).[2]

It is the divine educators, sent by God from time to time, who have forged humanity's moral consciousness. It certainly wasn't through the brutish exploits of great tyrants and conquerors of the past such as Genghis Khan, Alexander the Great, Julius Caesar, Napoleon, Hitler, or Stalin. Nor was it through the efforts of great political leaders, statesmen, and social activists such as Sun Yet-Sen, Thomas Jefferson, Benjamin Disraeli, and Mohandas Gandhi. Noted philosophers such as Socrates and Spinoza were unable to transform whole communities, replace hate with love in human hearts, alter attitudes and behavior, turn selfish people into selfless souls, or help people who seemed steeped in decadent ways to accept new moral standards.

Only the divine educators have been able to bring about the spiritual transformation of society. No one else in history has been able to transform society on such a grand scale. No sensible person will reject the notion that the transformative power manifested by the divine educators is not desperately needed now. The moral codes issued in the past lack the potency they possessed when they were revealed. There are simple and straightforward reasons for this.

Religious schism has resulted in conflicting dogma, thus obscuring the original teachings of the divine educators. Another reason is that most religionists, especially in the West, believe that humanity's moral consciousness was shaped by a single act in history—a super special divine revelation that revealed all that humankind needed to know to lead a righteous life—forever. That misconception has been the cause of a great deal of misunderstanding and misery in the world. In fact, failure to discern the unfolding evolutionary pattern of moral development through the ages has contributed mightily to humanity's present condition.

In reality, humanity's moral code is destined to evolve indefinitely. As humanity matures and advances, more advanced teachings are provided, much as in school. Students who refuse to accept anything but what they were taught in the second grade are going to find themselves in difficulty. Figuratively speaking, they are like thirteen year olds stuck in the second grade.

The evolution of the moral code is quickened whenever a divine educator appears. For example, Moses came to an unruly lot. In order to infuse in them a respect for moral discipline, he gave them the law in the form of the Mosaic Code, instructing them in Exodus 21:23–24: *"Thou shalt give life for life, eye for eye, tooth for tooth."* Based on today's ethical standards, the Mosaic Code may seem harsh and barbaric; but in fact this code established law and order among the Hebrews at a time when there was no humane system of jurisprudence and no penal system.

Thirteen hundred years later Jesus came to a more sophisticated people, who needed something more advanced than the Mosaic Code. So Jesus taught them that, instead of returning evil with evil, they should turn the other cheek and love their enemies. Thus the religion of God took a step forward. In addition to establishing a new set of moral principles, a divine educator reviews the teachings of previous divine educators. This is done to clarify the teachings of the past, enabling the recipients of the new teachings to gain a better understanding of why the new teachings are needed and an appreciation for the continuity of divine revelation.

While this process makes sense, opposition to the latest divine educator's claims creates so much havoc that the idea of the process is obscured by a storm of persecution and, at times, bodily harm or even martyrdom for him and his followers. But the persecution, no matter how fierce and bloody, cannot stop the will of God. The divine educators continue the process, providing new spiritual and moral guidelines. In their study of human social and spiritual evolution, some historians and sociologists have noticed a fascinating pattern that relates to the occurrence of a great spiritual reawakening.

In his four-volume work titled *Social and Cultural Dynamics*, the late Harvard sociologist Pitirim Sorokin stated that during periods of spiritual decline, materialism flourishes, plunging most people into a state of hedonism. The moral breakdown grows so severe that more and more people of all strata of society want to get off the materialistic roller coaster of disaster—they yearn to grow spiritually and become willing to abandon their hedonistic pursuits.

In time, Sorokin added, a charismatic mystical figure appears who sets off a collective spiritual resurgence based on a new set of values, and hearts are moved and minds enlightened. He cited the coming of figures such as Buddha and Jesus as examples of such figures. He also pointed out that attempts by scientists, economists, and philosophers to fill the spiritual void never take hold for an appreciable amount of time. Sorokin sensed that he was living at a time when the "sensate civilizations of the West" were dying and a spiritual reawakening was in the making. In his last volume Sorokin made a remarkably accurate prediction of how the fall of Western civilization will manifest itself.

Though Sorokin's vision was criticized greatly when it was shared, more than fifty years later the wise sociologist's prediction is presently being played out throughout the Western world, especially in the United States. Here are a few excerpts of what Sorokin foresaw in 1941:

> Rude force and cynical fraud will become the only arbiters of all values and of all interindividual and intergroup relationships. Might will become right. As a consequence, wars, revolutions, revolts, disturbances, brutality will be rampant. *Bellum omnium contra omnes*—man against man, class, nation, creed and race against class, nation and race—will raise its head.
>
> Freedom will become a mere myth for the majority and will be turned into an unbridled licentiousness by the

dominant minority. Inalienable rights will be alienated; Declarations of Rights either abolished or used as beautiful screens for an unadulterated coercion.

Governments will become more and more hoary, fraudulent, and tyrannical, giving bombs instead of bread; death instead of freedom; violence instead of law; destruction instead of creation. They will be increasingly short-lived, unstable and subject to overthrow.

The family as a sacred union of husband and wife, of parents and children will continue to disintegrate. Divorces and separations will increase until any profound difference between socially sanctioned marriages and illicit sex-relationships disappears. Children will be separated earlier and earlier from parents. The main sociocultural functions of the family will further decrease until the family becomes a mere incidental cohabitation of male and female while the home will become a mere overnight parking place mainly for sex-relationship.

The Sensate supersystem of our culture will become increasingly a shapeless "cultural dumping place," pervaded by syncretism of undigested cultural elements, devoid of any unity and individuality. Turning into such a bazaar, it will become prey of fortuitous forces making it an "object of history" rather than its self-controlling and living subject.

Its creativeness will continue to wane and wither. The place of Galileos and Newtons, Leibnitzes and Darwins, Kants and Hegels, Bachs and Beethovens, Shakespeares and Dantes, Raphaels and Rembrandts will be increasingly taken by a multitude of mediocre pseudo thinkers, science-makers, picture-makers, music-makers, fiction-makers, show-makers, one group more vulgar than the other. The place of moral categoric imperatives will be occupied by progressively atomistic and hedonistic devices of egotistic expediency, bigotry, fraud, and compulsion. The great Christianity will be replaced by a multitude of the most atrocious concoctions of fragments of science, shreds of philosophy, stewed in the inchoate mass of magical beliefs and ignorant superstitions. Constructive technological inventions will be supplanted progressively by destructive ones. . . .

In the increasing moral, mental and social anarchy and decreasing creativeness of Sensate mentality, the production of the material values will decline, depressions will grow worse, and the material standard of living will go down.

For the same reasons, security of life and possessions will fade. With these, peace of mind and happiness. Suicide, mental disease, and crime will grow. Weariness will spread over larger and larger members of the population.

Population will increasingly split into two types: the Sensate hedonists with their "eat, drink and love, for tomorrow we die;" and, eventually, into ascetics and stoics indifferent and antagonistic to Sensate values.

In this way Sensate culture and man will drift to their bankruptcy and self-destruction.[3]

10

Waiting for a Divine Educator

While humanity awaits deliverance from a condition that even the most celebrated humanitarians have been unable to alter, it is safe to say that most people are not likely to immediately recognize the divine educator when he appears. Superstitions and attachments to various scriptural interpretations would most likely veil the masses and their leaders from recognizing God's latest divine educator.

How do we know this is what would happen? Historically, this has always been the case, because it is what every divine educator has experienced. Some of the skepticism is understandable because people are naturally resistant to change, and there is always the fear of being fooled. Throughout the ages many charismatic individuals have claimed to be a divine educator, and many have drawn a small band of loyal and enthusiastic followers.

But in time, the impostors' true intentions have been exposed, and they have usually come to a miserable end. For example, in the eighth century, one of these misguided men known as Moses of Crete tried to walk from Greece to Israel by way of the sea. But the Mediterranean Sea didn't part, and he and many of his followers drowned. In more recent times, cult leader Jim Jones, claiming to be a messiah, created a so-called "heaven on earth" in Guyana. That "heaven on earth" turned out to be a paradise lost when Jones led over

107

nine hundred followers in a mass suicide. And then there was the pitiful episode of David Koresh, another self-proclaimed messiah, who led his followers, camped in their Waco, Texas, compound, to a fiery end in May of 1993 while trying to repulse federal forces.

Undoubtedly, the growing number of messianic impostors and spiritual fakirs has discouraged many people, including sincere seekers, from heeding the call of an authentic divine educator. No one wants to be fooled, especially those who have been fooled before. Perhaps the greatest pain a human being can experience results from the disillusionment of discovering that one's deeply held religious beliefs are false. The fear of making a mistake has left many people torn in conflict: On the one hand they yearn for some great figure to "save" them; on the other hand they don't know who to trust or which claim to embrace. As a consequence, they do nothing about exploring the claims.

It is important to note that despite the public's reluctance to investigate the message of the genuine divine educator, the fact that so many false prophets arise at the same time is proof that God's timing is right. If there were no demand for a spiritual way out of the difficulties people find themselves in, there would be no rash of religious opportunists pronouncing their preposterous claims.

In a way, the genuine divine educator can be likened to the sun and the impostors to the clouds that keep the public from seeing the sun. Just because the sun isn't seen doesn't mean it doesn't exist. In time, the clouds evaporate and some of the sun's rays begin to shine through, and people begin to notice.

So it has been with the divine educators. Usually after their passing, a greater number of people begin to embrace their message. This was certainly true of Jesus. Only a handful of people embraced his teachings during his lifetime, yet today Christianity is the most widespread religion in the world.

In Jesus's day and shortly after his crucifixion, the most influential and respected scholars in Israel and the Roman Empire discounted him and his followers as an eccentric group of powerless mischief-makers. In fact, during the second century, Tacitus, Rome's greatest historian at the time, felt the odd Jewish sect known as Christianity was a "corrupt superstitious belief," an "evil."[1]

Time is the most reliable test of the authenticity of a divine educator's claims. Impostors' efforts are short-lived. Their missions usually end when they die; whereas the divine educators' teachings take hold with a small segment of the population and spread after their passing, setting into motion the creation of a new civilization based on a new set of values and standards. But new divine teachings don't mean there will be no need for further revelations of God's will for humanity in the future. The divine teachings on which existing civilizations are based have become so badly distorted over the years that they often contribute to the social problems that beset humanity. In its search for answers that no human agency has been able to provide, humanity is subconsciously reaching out for help from the Divine. While there is little agreement as to what the solution to their woes is, there is plenty of agreement that something must be done soon to alleviate the mental and physical anguish that plague humanity today. It seems obvious that there is a desperate need for help from a source that is greater than any existing human agency.

Some daring souls are vocal about their expectations. Today a number of Christian sects sense Christ's return is near. Their evangelists proclaim from the pulpit that it is imminent. Other devout Christians await the appearance of the Spirit of Truth, for they are aware of what Jesus told his disciples at the Last Supper: *"I have yet many things to say unto you, but ye cannot bear them now. Howbeit when he, the Spirit of Truth, is come, he will guide you unto all truth."*(John 16:12) On Mt. Carmel, in Haifa, Israel, monks at the Carmelite monastery continue to watch the sky, waiting for Christ's second coming. There are references in the New Testament to Christ's returning to earth, which some interpret to mean he will come by way of a cloud (Matthew 24:30, Luke 21:27).

In 1992, the Lubavitchers, a major Hasidic Jewish sect, announced that the advent of the Messiah was at hand. Billboards throughout Israel urged Jews to prepare for the coming of the Messiah.

Clearly, an infusion of divine direction is desperately needed in the world today. We need new guidance that will enable humanity to deal with the unprecedented global challenges that face the human race. Nothing short of a new infusion of divine direction seems capable of overcoming the anxieties and desperate hopelessness encompassing the planet. What is needed is a message, Horace Holley writes, that "would consist of all the aspirations of the East as well as West, of women as well as men. Its newness, therefore, would appear in its supreme capacity to assimilate spiritual passion and social science into one human synthesis."[2] We need a message that will carry us through the next logical step in the social evolution of the planet. If we are objective in our assessment, it seems clear that the divine educators of the world's great religions have not provided such direction. This is not because of any limitation on their part, but simply because the people they came to educate were not ready to receive such guidance.

If we believe the world is in desperate need of a new divine educator and a new message that will address the problems of our time, we must ask ourselves a serious question: Is it possible that such a divine educator has already come?

11

New Light for Humanity

A divine educator has indeed already come. His name is Bahá'-u'lláh. Though he has come and gone, his message is still with us, given as a divine remedy to an ailing world.

That is quite a pronouncement, isn't it? I agonized over whether I should share it and if so, how. I know skeptics will find the concept of a new divine educator an anathema. Others will see it as heresy. Nonetheless, I feel compelled to share the news. After all, how could I withhold the message of the divine educator who is the source of most of the information I have shared up to this point? I certainly don't want to give the impression that whatever wisdom I have been able to communicate came from me. I am simply a vehicle for conveying some aspects of the divine educator's message.

Some of my advisors, women and men I respect, cautioned me against mentioning Bahá'u'lláh, worrying that it would be counterproductive. They felt that by revealing the source of the information, I would cancel out whatever good the readers might derive from the book. The name alone, a number of them warned, would probably scare the reader, especially those who are suspicious of anyone from the Middle East.

I pointed out to my friends that Jesus didn't come from Chicago or Moses from Houston. They countered by saying that most people are afraid of anything that gives the slightest impression that it might be considered cultish, especially a movement originating in the East. The fact that Bahá'u'lláh came from Iran compounds the problem, they said. Most people in the West associate Iran with fundamentalism, fanaticism, and terrorism.

I protested that Bahá'u'lláh is not a cult leader, that he is a divine educator and prophet like Jesus and Moses, the founder of an independent world religion that is more than 150 years old and which claims more than five million adherents living in more than 100,000 localities on every continent in the world.[1] I pointed out that members of the Bahá'í Faith in Iran are not associated with the present fanatical Iranian Islamic leadership, but are instead persecuted by that government. My advisors reminded me that the average person isn't aware of those facts and probably doesn't wish to know because they are suspicious of concepts and people who sound foreign and potentially threatening. They suggested that the instability and conflict in the Middle East would fuel suspicions and fears.

There were other reasons why my friends thought mentioning Bahá'u'lláh would invalidate everything I had said up to this point. They felt some readers would view the book with suspicion. They might see it as a vehicle to convert people to my religion, the Bahá'í Faith. They were concerned that some would see the book as an exercise in manipulation or an exploitation of people's vulnerabilities. They were afraid I would be accused by some critics of undermining other religions in order to promote the Bahá'í Faith.

It was difficult for me to listen my friends' concerns because I was aware of the tremendous suffering Bahá'u'lláh endured in order to share God's healing message with a despairing and moribund humanity. He was born into a Persian nobleman's family in 1817 and had every reason to look forward to a life of comfort, ease, and social and political status. Yet in his twenties, in obedience to God, he gave up all of that for a life marked by vilification, scorn, torture, exile, and imprisonment for the rest of his life. By choosing the path of suffering, Bahá'u'lláh—like Jesus and Moses—bowed to a will greater than his own. He did what he was directed to do, and now millions of people are benefiting from his sacrifices.

I knew that my friends and advisors had the best of intentions, and a lot of what they pointed out seemed to make practical sense. Nevertheless, I decided to follow my original impulse, taking my wife Carol's advice as to how I should proceed. "Be forthright," she said. "Explain why you agonized over this chapter, and share your honest intentions. Don't allow people's paranoia and prejudices prevent you from sharing the truth."

Had I yielded to my advisors' warnings, I would be guilty of withholding information that could be essential to a soul in pain. This was a condition I was all too familiar with. How could I withhold Bahá'u'lláh's healing message from others? I was clear about my motives. My intent was not to convert readers to my religion, but rather to help them become acquainted with their spiritual nature so that they could nurture it and become happier, more fulfilled human beings and, in turn, contribute more purposefully to the maintenance of a healthy community. If by applying Bahá'u'lláh's spiritual development principles to themselves they became better Christians, Muslims, and Jews, so be it. My paramount concern was to help others become more secure and clearly focused on the meaning of life. With that knowledge, I felt, they could make themselves happier and could help their community become a healthier place.

Although I do not want to discourage any readers who are genuinely interested in learning about the Bahá'í Faith from finding out more about its history and teachings, that is not the purpose of this book. There are many other books that provide that information. My purpose here is to provide Bahá'u'lláh's guidelines on how a person can become psychologically healthier and more spiritually fulfilled.

THINGS YOU CAN DO:

1. Begin to conscientiously pursue your own religious investigation, your own search for the truth. As has been pointed out, humanity is at a stage in its development where every individual is capable of recognizing the truth for himself or herself and to fighting their own spiritual battles. Without struggle, the truth is meaningless and there can be no real growth.

2. Discover and ponder the similarities of the world's great religions.

3. Ponder the simile that likens the religion of God to a school in which the students progress from one grade to the next based on the knowledge of the previous grade.

4. Consider the station of the divine educators versus that of religious leaders and great philosophers.

STEP FOUR   *Finding Our Spiritual Capacity*

STEP THREE   *Religion & the Divine Educators*

STEP TWO   *The Soul*

STEP ONE   *Oneness*

12

Finding Our Capacity for Spiritual Growth

Because the human being is composed of physical and spiritual aspects, both require continual nourishment and development if they are to function properly. When this doesn't happen, the person cannot fulfill his or her given capacity and inadvertently joins the growing number of dysfunctional individuals trying to survive in a dysfunctional society.

So the challenge we face as human beings is this: How do we develop both the spiritual and physical aspects of our nature to their fullest? In other words, how do we become truly balanced people, the kind of people we were meant to be? How do we attain this balance, which is essential to our individual health as well as to the health of the community? The answer is that the physical nature must become a willing servant of the soul. The remainder of this book will be devoted to how to achieve this.

In the majority of industrialized Western societies, most people have little trouble properly nourishing and caring for their bodies. Health fitness centers and the health food industry are doing a booming business. People are becoming more nutrition-conscious. Most of us make sure never to miss a wholesome breakfast, lunch, and dinner, and many of us have turned midmorning and afternoon snacks into a ritual.

Now, if the great majority of souls were to receive an equal amount of attention and the right kind of nourishment, the world wouldn't be facing the kinds of problems we are dealing with at present.

But before we can even consider what forms such spiritual attention and nourishment should take, it is essential that we accept the fact that there is a Creative Force, a Higher Power, or what most people refer to as God, Who loves the creation and wants what is best for us. God wants us to be happy. Some of us ask, "Then why doesn't God provide us with what we need?" The simple answer is that most of us don't know what is best for us. This is especially true when we do not know and love our Creator. When that happens, we are guided only by our physical nature. Without divine guidance, we become caught in the trap.

Certainly, God could make us all eternally happy in an instant. But such action would negate our humanness. Because of our Creator's abiding love and respect for us, we have been given certain distinctive characteristics including free will. We have been endowed with the potential to choose correctly, but making the right choices hinges on whether we turn toward God to receive divine guidance. When we don't, we are beset with a torrent of inner conflicts. If we abuse the privilege we call free will, using it only to fulfill physical desires, we render ourselves incapable of appreciating true freedom, which is attained through surrendering one's will to God's will.

Does that seem like a contradiction? It is a paradox that can't be fathomed by those whose orientation in life is purely materialistic. What is the meaning of this paradox? While we shouldn't ignore what's happening in the world, it is important to let go of certain materialistic attitudes and practices that hinder our spiritual growth. In other words, while we shouldn't run away from our responsibilities in this world by pursuing a monastic life, neither should we allow ourselves to be attached to the material things of this world. The world is a training ground for our spiritual development, and our training involves the discovery and development of our true self, a process that will help us to discover and develop the virtues latent within us.

Avoiding attachment to the things of this world doesn't imply that we should not appreciate the beauty around us or employ the time and energy-saving products of modern technology and enjoy a comfortable home. All of that is fine as long as it doesn't impede our spiritual development or hinder our desire to serve our fellow human beings and community through good deeds. However, there are certain steps we must take if we want to receive the divine guidance that will nurture our souls.

Simply being aware of our Higher Power's existence is not enough. Actually knowing and loving our Creator is essential. Fortunately, every human soul is equipped to do that, because we have the impulse to know, to love, and to be loved, and we can direct those impulses toward God. When we don't, we are like the man who is aware of a lamp in his room and never uses it, continuing instead to curse the darkness. Just as the man in the darkened room must take some action to gain some light, those of us who seek God's love must take some action in the form of expressing our love for God if we want to bring His spiritual light into our lives.

But loving God requires more than occasionally expressing a positive feeling in our heart for the Creator. What
prompts the feeling is important. If your feeling is based on
a belief in someone you respect, that is not a genuine expression of love for God. Nor is the feeling that stems from a
sincere desire to love God. The point is, you cannot love
what you do not know.

Regardless of what some people claim, no one, not even
the divine educators themselves, has engaged in a direct two-
way conversation with the Creator. Though our Higher Power's
love and presence is constant, no one is in direct contact with
It. If someone thinks she or he is, that person is suffering from
what Bahá'u'lláh calls "idle fancies and vain imaginings." God
is and will ever remain an unknowable essence.

So how do we get to know God? The only way it can
happen is through His divine educators. By immersing
ourselves in their teachings, we become acquainted with
the qualities of God and discover God's wishes for us. The
more we study these teachings, the more we begin to understand how they can be carried out. The greater our reliance on these teachings, the more we come to appreciate
God's will, which, on a personal level, is like knowing
someone's thoughts. And isn't that the most reliable way of
knowing another soul?

The benefits we derive from this exercise of getting to
know God through the divine educators move us to want
to know even more about God. So we turn to the divine
educators with greater eagerness and enthusiasm. The joy
that comes from enlightenment usually moves us to return to the source from which the enlightenment came. As a

consequence we intensify our pondering of the teachings that flow from the Creative Force through the divine educators.

It stands to reason that if we get to know God through the divine educators, then our messages to God in the form of prayers should be directed to the divine educators with whom we are most familiar. For me it is Bahá'u'lláh. For others, it may be Moses, Jesus, Muḥammad, Buddha, or Zoroaster. How my prayers reach God is a mystery. I don't know the mechanics of how prayers reach God or how divine guidance emanates from God to the divine educators. All I know is that, based on personal experience, my prayers are answered.

There are numerous, inexhaustible layers of meaning in the divine educators' teachings and writings. Only through consistent, sincere study do those meanings become apparent to us. Bahá'ís refer to the divine educators' teachings and writings as the Creative Word because of their mystical power. The more we understand them, the more we grow spiritually and thus grow closer to their Author. They have the power to create in us a new outlook on life; we become able to see and understand spiritual realities that we never saw or understood before. For example, we become more sensitive to others so that we can see beyond the mask of laughter of a troubled person and can see and feel his anguish and pain, just as I did with Josh. Every person has the capacity to attain such power, but attainment hinges on how far we progress in the process of knowing God.

As we learn to know and love God, thereby gaining a penetrative sight and the ability to hear the inner voice of those who are in pain, we gain something else that we grow to cherish. We become increasingly eager to take advantage of the opportunity to delve into the messages of the divine educators, seeking not only knowledge but also understanding. Members of the Bahá'í Faith call this process "deepening," referring to the fact that it deepens our knowledge and understanding of the teachings of the divine educators.

As we experience the transformative benefits of this exercise, we begin to feel the kind of need that a lover experiences when he is without his beloved. At this point we learn that we can no longer live without partaking of the divine educator's messages, and we willingly become involved in a lifelong, continuing process of knowing and loving God. In other words, the process evolves into a never-ending cycle of spiritual growth: The more we know God, the more we love God; and the more we love God, the more we want to know God. As the cycle continues, we become genuine lovers of God, experiencing an ineffable sense of exaltation whenever we open our heart to Him. It is a rapture best expressed for me by Bahá'u'lláh:

By Thy glory! Every time I lift up mine eyes unto Thy heaven, I call to mind Thy highness and Thy loftiness, and Thine incomparable glory and greatness; and every time I turn my gaze to Thine earth, I am made to recognize the evidences of Thy power and the tokens of Thy bounty. And when I behold the sea, I find that it speaketh to me of Thy majesty, and of the potency of Thy might, and of Thy sovereignty and Thy grandeur. And at whatever time I contemplate the mountains, I am led to discover the ensigns of Thy victory and the standards of Thine omnipotence.

I swear by Thy might, O Thou in Whose grasp are the reins of all mankind, and the destinies of the nations! I am so inflamed by my love for Thee, and so inebriated with the wine of Thy oneness, that I can hear from the whisper of the winds the sound of Thy glorification and praise, and can recognize in the murmur of the waters the voice that proclaimeth Thy virtues and Thine attributes, and can apprehend from the rustling of the leaves the mysteries that have been irrevocably ordained by Thee in Thy realm.[1]

Spiritual constancy requires self-discipline. Have you ever heard of an Olympic runner who didn't train regularly or a famous concert violinist who didn't practice daily? Most likely you haven't. It takes more than raw talent to become successful as an athlete, artist, or dancer; regular conditioning and practice are required. Without it, the performer will inevitably falter, regardless of her or his potential. The same is true of a person who yearns to grow spiritually.

Prayer and deepening in the divine educator's writings are to the seeker of spiritual development as calisthenics and daily running are to a 1,500-meter champion, or as practice is to a world-class jazz saxophonist. If a person wishes to grow spiritually, he or she must be in good spiritual condition. This depends on personal discipline, which many of us resist because we feel it requires too much effort. Perhaps it seems to restrict our freedom, and we may doubt that we can do it, even though we have done it in the past, not realizing we were exercising self-discipline.

For example, today we brush our teeth regularly. Though that hygienic practice is done routinely now, there was probably a time when we resisted it, complaining that it was a waste of time. The same is true with washing before eating. Today, not brushing our teeth or not washing our hands before we eat a meal would be a departure from our lifestyle that would make us feel uncomfortable.

The same thing can happen with prayer and deepening. Chances are that it will require considerable effort initially to integrate prayer and deepening into our daily schedule, but if we are diligent, eventually we will find we miss it sorely if for some reason we are unable to pray or deepen one day. The day will feel incomplete; we will most likely feel uneasy, more tense than usual.

Sandy, a thirty-seven-year-old mother of two, had worked long and hard on integrating prayer and deepening into her daily routine. One day she learned what happens when the pattern is broken or interrupted.

She had just returned from dropping cupcakes off at her son's school and making a quick trip to the grocery store. She knew she was running late. She parked the car in the drive, loaded her arms with groceries, and had just put them down in the kitchen when the doorbell rang. It was Ann Marie, a woman she had met at a PTA meeting. They had gotten into a discussion about spirituality (Ann Marie had admitted that spirituality was the furthest thing from her mind) and had formed a budding friendship.

They had decided to meet every Thursday afternoon at 2:00 to discuss their views. It was Thursday, and Sandy was not in the mood for any spiritual discussion. She had had a horrendous morning. All she wanted to do was to be alone. She even thought of feigning a headache, but Ann Marie was there at the door, and to lie and turn her away would have been rude. Sandy thought she would try to cut the discussion short, make some excuse.

She went to the door, opened it, put a smile on her face, and invited Ann Marie into the kitchen so Sandy could put the groceries away. Ann Marie sat on a stool at the island while Sandy took groceries out of bags, banging cupboards open and shut. In her haste to get rid of her friend she accidentally dropped a carton of eggs, making a terrible mess on the floor. That was the last straw. Sandy let out an exasperated sound, stomped over to the closet, and got out a mop and bucket.

"Whoa! Sandy! Calm down!" Ann Marie took the mop and bucket out of her hands and put them aside. Then she took her friend by the arm and sat her down at the stool next to her. "Have a seat. I'll make some tea while you tell me what's wrong. You're acting like I usually do when I'm stressed out."

Sandy took a deep breath and began a recitation of her day. The mother in charge of special occasions in her son's class had waited until the last minute to ask Sandy for the two dozen cupcakes, calling her at 9:30 last night. So she got up at her usual hour of 6:30 and baked the cupcakes. While they were in the oven she packed the kids' lunches, got them ready for school, walked them down to the bus stop, got in her car to do errands, and as soon as she backed out of the driveway, the muffler fell off. She went back in the house, changed into grubby clothes, called the repair shop, gathered tools, got under the car and wired the muffler up with a coat hanger, and noisily drove to the repair shop. Of course, all of that had taken two hours that she didn't have and had put her behind schedule by two hours.

By now the tea was finished. Ann Marie poured her friend a cup and said, "You usually take things in stride. Why is this day any different?"

Sandy thought back over her morning. It didn't take her long to realize what had gone wrong. "I didn't say my morning prayers and read from the sacred writings. I baked cupcakes instead." The realization made Sandy smile. "Thanks, Ann Marie. If you hadn't cared and sensed my uneasiness and asked me about it, I would never have figured out why I was so edgy."

Sandy and Ann Marie shared some prayers and went on to talk about what had happened. Ann Marie was extremely impressed with the change in her friend's demeanor. Sandy's face had just lit up, her posture had improved, and her breathing had slowed. A physical change was clearly visible. Ann Marie asked Sandy about her daily routine of prayer and meditation, and within a few weeks she too had integrated these steps into her own daily routine. After a few months it had become so much a part of her that she didn't feel right or complete without it.

Finding the time to pray and deepen seems to be one of our greatest problems. Because we live in a society that doesn't give much recognition to the spiritual aspect of our nature but gives an inordinate amount of attention to the development of our bodies, it's easy to neglect ourselves spiritually. We know what happens to us physically when we don't eat properly, don't exercise, and don't sleep enough: We become more susceptible to disease, we weaken and tire easily, and we more quickly feel the effects of aging.

Driving God out of our consciousness has a similar effect on us spiritually, except that the deterioration process isn't as discernible. Physical neglect can be detected in a mirror, by a physician, or by other people such as our relatives, friends, or coworkers. But because most of the people around us are generally in a comparable spiritual condition, they are unable to detect the effects of our spiritual neglect. When we neglect to nourish ourselves spiritually, life grows more frightening, more uncertain as we search for ever greater, more pleasurable material comforts, feeling that perhaps through them we will find happiness.

The more we grow spiritually, the more committed we are to our involvement in the growth process. But for most of us, getting started is difficult. There are many material distractions, some of which we have already mentioned. Perhaps for those living in the West, employing a systematic approach would help them start and sustain their spiritual development since they may already be engaged in such an approach to caring for their bodies.

Our meal schedule offers a prime example. Most of us usually eat breakfast at the same time each day. We probably also eat something during a coffee break a couple of hours later, then consume more food at roughly the same time each day for lunch. Perhaps we have a snack during the afternoon coffee break. Then there is supper, and after supper, the daily cycle is probably completed with a bedtime snack. For 365 days a year we follow the same eating pattern, deviating from the pattern only rarely. When it's necessary to change our routine, we may grumble and become irritable or uncommunicative. So we make sure we maintain the system.

Although we know it is important to seek balance in our lives—and that means developing both aspects of our nature— in the long run, the spiritual aspect tends to be more important to us, for there will come a time when our body disintegrates, and we are left in the world of the spirit for eternity.

What can we do to systemize our spiritual development? This is a question I had to wrestle with when I discovered my spiritual reality and began to understand how I had neglected its development for so long. Realizing how essential it was, I made a commitment to becoming involved in a spiritual development process.

When I started the process, I had no idea it would become a lifelong commitment. Interestingly, the decision wasn't something I forced myself to make. After a while the benefits were so remarkable that I decided I couldn't live without the process. The thought of being cut off from it became my greatest fear. Perhaps that's what is meant by the fear of God.

As I attempted to create a workable systematic process for myself, I found the physical and spiritual nourishment metaphor helpful. Without a wholesome eating pattern and a healthful diet, I knew my physical well-being would suffer. Over the years, I have had to make adjustments to what and how I eat. Gaining knowledge from competent physicians and nutritionists helped me organize a regimen that so far has produced a healthy body. Obviously, awareness of the source of knowledge for creating a spiritual development process is also necessary. Through the ages the divine educators have provided that guidance.

As a Bahá'í, I turn to Bahá'u'lláh for direction. Sincere and open-minded Christians and Jews can find similar directions from the founders of their faiths.

Just as I do certain things daily in order to maintain my physical health, there are certain things I do daily to maintain my spiritual health, but the latter isn't as easy as the former. Brushing my teeth, showering, and eating three meals every day had long been a necessary routine before I became involved in a spiritual development process. Introducing new activities into a firmly established thirty-year-old behavioral pattern was a shock to my system. It took me outside my comfort zone.

While intellectually I could accept the need to become involved in a systematic process of spiritual development, emotionally I resisted the changes I knew I needed to make, often resorting to rationalization to avoid doing what I knew was the right thing to do. This internal battle went on for several years, gradually decreasing in intensity with the passage of time until it finally faded away and I found myself in cherished compliance with what I knew was best for me. I now know what religious thinkers mean by the term "rebirth."

However, spiritual rebirth, like birth, is not a static condition. Just as an infant requires continual nourishment to grow, those who experience spiritual rebirth understand that their new condition is really an ongoing process; they must continue to follow the path that led to their new spiritual condition. It is a sign of spiritual rebirth when we no longer view the process as a duty and see it instead as a precious privilege. When this happens, we pursue the process with greater passion, which in turn accelerates our spiritual growth.

When we follow such a course faithfully, the soul finds itself gaining access to God's storehouse of divine powers. Our intuition becomes sharper, and we develop a penetrative sight that enables us to see the reality of others. As a result we become able to help those who are afraid to share their burdens with others. Our energy level for service to others soars. We willingly become a channel for God's grace, and we experience the benefits of divine assistance.

I feel my father-in-law, Curtis Kelsey, was such a man. He never attained great worldly prominence, though he worked hard and efficiently as a self-made engineer who designed and built pipelines for power, water, and chemical companies.

Though he was a product of a well-to-do family, Curtis Kelsey dropped out of school in the eighth grade, becoming a pool room hustler as a youth. An astounding spiritual experience in 1917 drew him to the spiritual path, from which he rarely strayed.

One day while working in the woods in the Berkshire Mountains in Massachusetts, Curtis's head began to hurt. He thought it was probably just a headache and continued to work. But the pain intensified, and after a night of restless sleep it still didn't subside. His body began to ache and was seized by chills. For several days he worked, unable to drive off the pain. Finally he had to go home. The doctor who examined him said it was a good thing he didn't stay much longer in the Berkshires because he had contracted typhoid fever. About all he could do was to wait the disease out in bed. The headaches persisted. One night the aching and pounding were so severe that not even the ice pack his mother had given him could dull the pain. Frustrated, Curtis buried his head in his pillow, crying for relief. Suddenly, the pain vanished, and the most wondrous music he had ever heard filled the room. Curtis turned, straining to see in the dark if people were around him playing instruments. But it was music that could only come from a great symphony orchestra. He lay back for a moment, being listening by sounds so beautiful it didn't matter where they came from. His whole being was bathed in a magnificent feeling of well-being. He had to share this wonder with someone. He called his mother. As he began to sit up, the music began to fade.

When Mrs. Kelsey entered the room, the music disappeared. She turned the light on and found her son sitting up, relaxed, with a look of wonderment on his face.

"Mother," he said, "the strangest thing happened."

"What was it?"

"I heard the most beautiful music."

"Music?"

"Yes . . . coming from some great orchestra."

She moved closer to him, placing a hand on his forehead, thinking that perhaps his fever had driven him into delirium.

"No. . . there's nothing wrong with me, Mother," he said.

"What about your headache?"

"When the music came it went away."

Mrs. Kelsey looked at her son for several seconds, then said, "Maybe we can find the answer to your experience in the Bahá'í writings." She went to her room to fetch a book, pulled up a chair to Curtis, and they started reading passages from Bahá'u'lláh. Curtis couldn't turn away from the book. "Mother, why have you not told me about these writings before?"

"I have tried for nine years," she said, "but you didn't show any interest."

Mrs. Kelsey turned to a passage and read it aloud: "God screens us evermore from premature ideas . . . our eyes cannot see things that stare us in the face until the hour arrives when the mind is ripened. Then we behold them, and the time when we saw them not is like a dream."[2]

Curtis's knowledge and love of God grew until his faith became the most important thing in his life. As a result he found himself in a position of drawing divine power to solve worldly problems. This is a position that all humans are capable of attaining, but few succeed in doing so.

Curtis knew that involvement in the spiritual development process wouldn't shield him from problems. In fact, as he matured spiritually, he viewed each problem—and there were many in his life—as a test meant to refine his character and reinforce his reliance on God in seeking solutions.

Many of his friends and relatives were amazed at the form those solutions took. Those who were not religious attributed them to strange circumstances or to serendipity, and the more spiritually minded viewed them as miracles. To Curtis, the dramatic solutions a fact of life, part of a pattern of cause and effect available to everyone. Throughout his adult life he seemed to be rescued from one impending disaster after another. His daughters remember them, especially one instance.

During the Great Depression in the 1930s, business was so poor that Curtis was forced to lay off most of the staff of the Continental Pipe Company, which he headed. He was functioning as the chief engineer, salesman, and production supervisor. During the summer, he would take his four children and wife on a monthlong business trip through New England in his black 1932 Buick. Between business calls, he would visit old friends, which the children enjoyed. They also liked sleeping in their big tent and eating outdoors around a bonfire.

One night, after another disappointing day of work, Curtis was looking for a place to camp. The spot he found seemed ideal. There were no thorny bushes or trees to block the view of the star-filled sky, and the pleasant breeze was a relief from the hot, humid day on the road. But around dawn, some of the children got up earlier than usual, for there was a terrible odor permeating the tent. When they dashed out and quickly surveyed the area, they discovered they had camped on the edge of a town garbage dump. Evidently, the breeze had shifted during the night. It didn't take long to pack up and get out of that place.

Perhaps in his haste to leave, Curtis had not tied the tent securely onto the back of the car, for it fell off while he was driving. When he retrieved it, it was ruined, full of large holes. This was a dilemma. He had only enough money for a few more meals, and now they had no overnight shelter. And he needed to be on the road for another five days because there were more business calls to make. Not only that—there wasn't enough money to return home. Though the family prayed every day, they prayed harder after losing the tent.

Curtis believed God would answer his plea for help. How? He didn't know. But he was sure God would answer.

Back on the road, and after two unsuccessful business stops, Curtis started hunting for a place to spend the night, a place that would protect his family from the elements. He finally found a spot—a gully with a clear stream. In a matter of minutes, Curtis had a fire going, and his wife, Harriet, scraped up enough food for the family's last hot meal. While cooking, she asked the children to wash for supper, and they scampered to the stream. On the way they discovered six or seven colorful objects on the ground with a lot of quarters around them. They were machines, and as they pulled the knobs more coins shot out of them. The eldest daughter ran back to her parents with a handful of quarters and explained what they had found.

Curtis got enough money from the abandoned casino slot machines to buy a new tent and purchase enough food and gasoline for the remainder of the trip. But the Kelsey family's sudden good fortune didn't end with the discovery of a pot of cash; Curtis secured a contract to build a pipeline from the last business he called on.

13

The Portrait of an Ideal Human Being

While Curtis Kelsey treated the money his family found in their time of need as yet another everyday occurrence, he worked at being the recipient of divine assistance. However, he didn't consider it work, but rather an act of love, because the effort he put forth provided him with pleasure.

How does one attain such a state of spiritual development? It is not through human initiative alone or by following through on a personal good idea. That won't do it. It is discovering and carrying out the guidelines to spiritual development provided by a divine educator. In Curtis's case it was a matter of applying the teachings of Bahá'u'lláh to every aspect of his life.

Before engaging in the spiritual development process, it is best to be aware of what the commitment will lead to, for this awareness will provide the incentive to pursue the process. Bahá'u'lláh offers a portrait of the qualities we can develop through this endeavor. It is essentially a set of goals in the form of an open appeal:

Be generous in prosperity, and thankful in adversity. Be worthy of the trust of thy neighbor, and look upon him with a bright and friendly face. Be a treasure to the poor, an admonisher to the rich, an answerer of the cry of the

needy, a preserver of the sanctity of thy pledge. Be fair in
thy judgment, and guarded in thy speech. Be unjust to no
man, and show all meekness to all men. Be as a lamp unto
them that walk in darkness, a joy to the sorrowful, a sea
for the thirsty, a haven for the distressed, an upholder and
defender of the victim of oppression. Let integrity and
uprightness distinguish all thine acts. Be a home for the
stranger, a balm to the suffering, a tower of strength for
the fugitive. Be eyes to the blind, and a guiding light unto
the feet of the erring. Be an ornament to the countenance
of truth, a crown to the brow of fidelity, a pillar of the
temple of righteousness, a breath of life to the body of
mankind, an ensign of the hosts of justice, a luminary
above the horizon of virtue, a dew to the soil of the human heart, an ark on the ocean of knowledge, a sun in the
heaven of bounty, a gem on the diadem of wisdom, a
shining light in the firmament of thy generation, a fruit
upon the tree of humility.[1]

I know that after reading such a portrait, many people
would feel incapable of achieving that degree of perfection.
I remember feeling that way.

Fortunately, I resisted the part of me that fears change,
and I made an attempt. It was one of the best decisions I
have ever made, for I gained a perspective that has become a
helpful guide in my life: Almost anything is attainable if you
know what you want, have the tools to achieve it, and—
most importantly—the patience to stay the course. Once I
understood this concept, I realized that I wasn't expected to

achieve overnight what Bahá'u'lláh describes. What is most important is making a consistent effort, which will bring about steady growth.

Obviously, attaining the attitude and behavior that Bahá'u'lláh describe in the portrait requires considerable effort, especially in the beginning, when materialistic habits are in conflict with the new spiritual practices we are trying to adopt. The tug of the old ways is hard to resist.

For most of us the conflict becomes an ongoing battle. But with faith, patience, persistence, and a vision of what the struggle leads to, the intensity of the conflict lessens and the spiritual development process becomes easier. With time and persistence, eventually we reach a stage where we have greater control over the old habits. Furthermore, as we gain experience, we recognize what has led to our newfound freedom, our sense of exaltation. As a consequence, we are inspired to continue our involvement in the process of spiritual development. We begin to know that we could never resume the old habits and that the only safeguard against reverting to them is to continue the spiritual development process. The promise of further growth gives us incentive not to abandon the process. Eventually, we reach a point when the will to continue isn't as difficult to maintain because we have experienced such benefits that we await future bounties with great expectation. In time, we realize that we are involved in a lifelong process that we are unwilling to abandon.

With new insights born from involvement in the spiritual development process, we realize that the greatest tragedy confronting humanity is not what the obvious problems of racism, sexism, violence, drugs, economic troubles, wars, religious strife, or crime. These are simply the tragic symptoms of the disease that is ailing humankind.

The real tragedy is that the great majority of the planet's population remains unaware of their spiritual reality and does not know what it takes to develop their spiritual potentialities.

THINGS YOU CAN DO:

1. Read from the Word of God every morning and evening. It is available from many sources, including the Bhagavad-Gita, the Bible, the Koran, the Bahá'í writings, and other holy books. It doesn't have to be a long passage. What matters most is the quality of your attention. Reflect on what you read. This is food for the soul.

2. Pray daily, remembering that God is always available. Take all of your problems to Him. Curtis Kelsey internalized this principle, freeing himself from fear and anxiety and providing him with a clearer view of reality.

3. Study the life of the founder of your religion. Try to use unfamiliar sources so that you develop a deeper and broader understanding of the divine educator's contributions to humanity's spiritual and social development. In your prayers, seek his help.

4. Try to organize a daily spiritual development program, selecting the appropriate site, books, and time for personal deepening.

STEP FIVE *Tools for Developing Our True Self*

STEP FOUR *Finding Our Spiritual Capacity*

STEP THREE *Religion & the Divine Educators*

STEP TWO *The Soul*

STEP ONE *Oneness*

14

The Battle between Our False Self and True Self

Though the steps toward spiritual development are few and simple, they aren't easily integrated into our lives, given the daily pressures we face and the habits we develop over time.

Before we take the steps necessary to develop spiritually, it is essential that we make a commitment to discovering who we really are. To make that commitment, understanding the composition of self is necessary. There is the "false self" and the "true self." The false self is a collection of pretenses, wishful thinking, and the result of familial modeling and social stimuli, which our conscious mind has embraced as its reality. This conscious reality becomes the anchor for all of our decisions and choices, but ultimately it keeps us in the trap. Fear fuels the false self, and its greatest fear is the loss of comfort and safety that we have labored to create to avoid the pains and hurts of the past.

The true self, as you have surely guessed, is the soul, our unconscious reality and our connection with God. Goodness and unconditional love emanate from the soul. Our unconscious reality is pure, laden with divine qualities that are just waiting to be discovered and developed. Ideally, the conscious reality and unconscious reality must merge, so that we can become internally unified. However, this merging cannot come about without continuous effort and sustained internal work on the part of the individual, and this takes commitment. Though all of the divine educators have urged their followers to "know thyself," many of us haven't taken the appeal to heart, and others simply don't know how. As a result, when we try to follow the steps of spiritual development, it is like trying to paint a surface marred by barnacles and rust. The experienced painter knows that for the paint to stick, the rust and barnacles must be removed.

To become aware of what is festering in our unconscious is going to take lots of prayer and effort. Why? Because digging into the unconscious and drawing to the conscious mind the memories we would prefer not to confront can be a painful process. This often means breaking out of denial.

Yet it is important to note that in most instances pain is a catalyst for spiritual growth. Although nobody seeks out experiences that generate pain, if the pain results from our efforts to grow spiritually, we should be willing to bear it, for like childbirth, the end result makes everything worthwhile. The point is, when we attempt to identify the past hurts that we have repressed in our unconscious mind, we will discover that the unconscious mind isn't the repository of all evil impulses, as we may have been led to believe.

On the contrary, according to spiritually oriented psychiatrists like M. Scott Peck, the unconscious mind is a repository of all that is good.[1] Because of this, we sense it is a safe place and instinctively use it to hide what we are ashamed of and what is too painful to acknowledge. In reality, the unconscious mind is the vast part of the soul that we were never aware of; our conscious mind is, in a sense, just the tip of the iceberg. As we grow spiritually we become acquainted with more and more of what is in the unconscious mind. The experience energizes us, and we gain the will and the courage to deal with what we have repressed. The conscious mind, which has been shaped by society, takes on more and more of the characteristics of the unconscious. By faithfully developing the soul's powers and latent qualities, the conscious mind grows and the unconscious shrinks. As this process continues, there may come a time when the unconscious fades completely into the conscious mind. When this happens, every thought is laced with the love of God.

Considering what it takes to know oneself, it is easy to understand why 'Abdu'l-Bahá, the eldest son of Bahá'u'lláh and chief interpreter of his father's teachings, called our life in the here and now a workshop and not an art gallery.[2] Knowing oneself requires consistent treading into areas we prefer to avoid lest we uncover and relive unpleasant experiences.

Perhaps we were abused by people close to us such as our parents, teachers, or religious leaders. Not that our parents were conscious of being abusive. In many instances the abuse stemmed from an incorrect understanding of human nature, which led to psyche-wounding child-rearing practices that were universally accepted at the time as the best way to rear children. Two major principles of these practices come to mind: "A child is to be seen and not heard" and "Spare the rod, spoil the child."

Of course, not all of the abuses we may have suffered were physical; many were emotional and spiritual—like abandonment. Abandonment could mean being left with a relative or friend and never seeing your parents again. But for the most part it has to do with parents' not providing a child with the necessary attention, direction, affection or not being available when the child needs to share something important with someone she or he trusts and loves. Spending more time at work than at home can be a form of abandonment. When this happens on a regular basis, children learn that their parents' work is more important than they are. Because the children love their parents, they develop ways to avoid thinking about the choice their parents have made. One way they do this is to repress their feelings of betrayal and resentment. The hurt is buried in the unconscious mind, and the child grows into adulthood having developed a wall between his present and past realities. The wall is so effective that he can't remember his childhood hurts.[3]

Whether we'll admit it or not, most of us as children buried many hurts in our unconscious. These hurts don't remain dormant. Over time they shape and influence our behavior as adults. Many of our shortcomings and emotional weaknesses stem from those carefully concealed childhood hurts. To overcome these shortcomings and weaknesses, we need to know their origin. Without that knowledge, we cannot heal ourselves.

Any competent healer realizes that achieving a cure is dependent on knowing the cause of the ailment. So in this day and age, the spiritual call to "know thyself" is to bring to full awareness what has been moving us and to rethink and rebuild it on a spiritual foundation. This doesn't mean building on what is already there. Doing that would only push deeper into the unconscious mind what we are ashamed of revealing to ourselves and others. The rust and barnacles must be removed before the paint can really stick.

A process of readjustment and reorientation is required. This process can be compared to releasing a poison we have accumulated through painful experiences we didn't choose to have. The challenge of knowing oneself in this day and age is, grappling with our conscious reality, bringing our unconscious reality to consciousness, and uniting the two.

I could not have done this by myself. I needed help from others, especially those who were deeply involved in the struggle to "know thyself." I benefited from their personal struggle, their heart-to-heart encouragement, and their kind empathy, but their assistance wasn't enough. The greatest help came from a power far greater than myself or my friends and associates. That help came from God. There was no way I could have broken down the thick and stubborn door to my past without God's help. His greatest help was to point the way. Had God not urged us to "know thyself," I would never have made the effort to break the hold my false self had on me and become acquainted with my true self. I was willing to heed God's appeal because I had grown to love Him. There was no question in my mind about why He made the appeal: It was to help me and everyone else to fulfill our potential as human beings.

It is interesting that the more awareness I became of what had been festering in my unconscious, the more willing I was to endure the pain of discovering the truth. It was worth enduring because, for the first time in my life, I was becoming aware of why I behaved and felt the way I did most of the time. I was gaining my freedom, freedom from the bondage of my false self. This freedom felt so good that I was willing to endure the pain involved in getting to it. With the knowledge I was gaining about my past hurts, I found myself in a much better position to correct the faults in me that others deemed unattractive. I was able to identify many of my own shortcomings, acknowledge them, and, with God's guidance, begin to overcome them.

How grateful I am for the breakthrough, for without it, I would have continued to try harder and harder to pretend to be someone I really wasn't. To avoid dealing with my vulnerabilities, I had created a fantasy I had forced myself to believe was reality. Thank God for the breakthrough, for only then was I able to gain an appreciation of true freedom. Genuine freedom is won when the unconscious reality is unlocked, released, and integrated into our consciousness. The longer we hide from the pain and shame of the past, the more we understand why we behave and feel the way we do. As a consequence, we are no longer living a lie, and we are able to work at overcoming the pain of unhealed wounds sustained as a child. When this happens, we are on our way to attaining balance.

For years, I paid little or no attention to heeding the divine educators' appeal to "know thyself." Oh, I had read numerous times Bahá'u'lláh's warning that *"True loss is for him whose days have been spent in utter ignorance of his self."*[4] But I did nothing in response to the warning. It simply wasn't on my list of high priorities, mainly because I was convinced that I didn't need to engage in such an exercise. There were far more important challenges for me, like helping to save the world. You see, I believed I already had a sound understanding of who I was. After all, I had achieved some success professionally, not only in journalism but in education as well, and I had written eleven books and produced a number of television documentaries. I thought of myself as an "achiever," "a man of action," and I was proud of that reputation. I also had a stable family. Not many men could say that they had been married to the same woman for thirty-eight years and had never cheated on her. I had four successful children—all of them dedicated servants of humankind— of whom I was very proud. Ours was viewed by many as the ideal family, and I took pride that I had played a significant role in making it so.

I considered myself a religious person, devoted to my faith, someone who worked hard at living by its tenets. It meant a great deal to me, though I would never admit it publicly nor even to those who were closest to me, that it was important to me to be respected by people I considered to be highly accomplished. Managing to attain their respect brought me some contentment in life.

But there was another side of myself that I refused to explore. It was the dark side. Whenever someone, including my wife, tried to get me to look at it for my own good, I would grow defensive. Those who persisted, I felt, were trying to embarrass or humiliate me. Maybe jealousy and envy were driving them, I would think. I fought back because I didn't want anyone to destroy the cocoon of contentment I had worked so hard to create for myself. When someone found fault with me or disagreed with me, I would view them as my enemy and avoid having anything to do with them. It was my way of psychologically eliminating a potential threat.

The only thing that restrained me from loathing and conspiring against my imagined enemies was my love of God. The love was so intense that I was afraid of violating God's spiritual principles and breaking divine laws. One of my toughest tests was trying to love my enemies. It was a continuous tug-of-war between my battered and sensitive ego and my true self.

The only critic I never viewed as an enemy was my wife. Because I loved her, I couldn't avoid her, at least not for long. There were moments when I would hide away, burying myself in my work. I didn't know how to deal with criticism from someone I loved. From time to time we had arguments, but this was something I tried to avoid. My parents had argued a lot, and I didn't want my marriage marred by spousal disputes. Besides, there was our image to uphold. My hope was usually that in a day or two all would be forgotten and forgiven. And that's what usually happened. To avoid further unpleasantness I devised a way to avoid arguments. When my wife and I talked on an emotional level, I would give the impression of listening wholeheartedly, acknowledging what she was saying about me with a continual affirmative nod of my head. What I was actually doing was giving her an opportunity to vent. I wasn't about to take her criticism of me to heart, even though it was given in the spirit of love. She was trying to encourage me to break through the wall I had built over the years that separated my false self from my true self. She had already made the breakthrough and wanted her husband, the man she chose to love, to experience the freedom she was experiencing. But I resisted her urgings in the least combative way possible, and she sensed my resistance notwithstanding my insistence to the contrary. She grew sad, and that in turn saddened me. I didn't want to cause her unhappiness. Nothing I did—all of it superficial, like taking her out to dinner or spending a week together in Florida—could shake the sadness she was trying to hide from me. It seemed like we were drifting apart, and that scared me.

For several months I tried to pray about the problem, but that was difficult. I couldn't bring myself to pray, because my motives weren't pure. I had been trying to manipulate my wife to avoid looking honestly at myself. I was afraid. She was crying more than ever before. Though I knew intellectually that the tears were a part of the interior healing process she was undergoing, the idea of crying scared me. Why resurrect old hurts, open old wounds, I thought. Why waste time trying to relive the past when there was so much to do today, and there was always tomorrow.

My rationalizations didn't relieve my anxieties, nor did they overcome the differences between me and my wife. In desperation I fell to my knees, still burdened with my questionable motives and all of my imperfections, and I cried out for help.

I believe God answered my prayer by infusing my wife with the courage, determination, and patience to continue challenging me and to remain firm in her insistence that I wasn't really listening to her. In time, my defenses broke down. Because I couldn't fool the person I loved most in this world, I could no longer fool myself. My breakthrough wasn't spontaneous; it was more like a chipping away process. Even when I decided to gain an awareness of my true self and fully cooperated with my wife, there were times when I reverted to old behavioral patterns. At first I wasn't aware of into the patterns, but as I ventured further and further into my past, I began to understand what was shaping my conscious reality. I found myself developing a more wholesome attitude, and I learned to spot it when I reverted to old patterns or felt an inclination to do so. After a while the manipulation to which I had resorted before were no longer a part of my being.

As I reflect on the path I chose to find and develop my true self, I realize the struggle has been both painful and joyful. I learned that God is aware of our unconscious prayers. Mercifully, God hears our innermost pleas, even those that we may not be aware of on a conscious level, for denial of our unconscious reality prevents us from hearing the yearnings of the child within us.

I believe that my decision to take the time and pretend to listen wholeheartedly to my wife during our talks was God's answer to the plea of the child within me. Though outwardly I was listening to make her happy and inwardly I was resisting her message, some of what she said seeped through my defenses. It forced me to think, even only for a moment or two, about issues I had refused to consider before. With the passage of time, the things my wife was telling me garnered more and more of my attention. To sort out what I was learning, I spent a year in a group therapy program.

I learned what went into the creation of my false self and what drove me to create it. I had a need to forget most of my childhood, for it had been a time of deep pain and disappointment. While I loved my parents, I didn't like what they were doing to me, to themselves, and to my sister and brother. My parents were continually arguing, unlike the ideal parents I saw in the movies. There were times when I wished I belonged to one of those families on the screen and not to my own.

My father had a volcanic temper. I shuddered every time he screamed, smashed his big fist on the kitchen table, or threw a plate against the wall. Being whipped with his "cat o' nine tails" wasn't as painful to me as the fact that he didn't take the time to play with me, to help me with my homework, attend my games, or find out what I was interested in. He never asked me what I would like to be when I grew up. I kept telling him what I wanted to be. It was always something like a doctor or a lawyer, because I knew he respected lawyers and doctors. I couldn't share my dreams with him because I was afraid he would ridicule me. I tried hard to find out what he wanted me to be. Since he was very mechanical, I volunteered to help him, even as an eight-year-old. I did this to get close to him, to have an opportunity to make him proud of me. But in his eyes I could never do anything right. As a result, I always approached every assignment with the fear of failing. It was a terrible feeling. But even worse was his wrath when I would fail. "Idiot," he would shout. And there were times when he would call me "worthless," or say that I "wouldn't amount to anything." Then when I shied away from helping him, he would call me "lazy" or a "bum."

My father ridiculed my involvement in athletics, declaring time and time again that I was wasting my time "hitting a ball with a stick." But I had to play ball, for it was the only way I could gain some respect; it was also a means of staying away as much as possible from a home full of argument, anger, bitterness, and sadness.

In my childhood home, I was just another person to feed and clothe. There was never any heart-to-heart communication. I felt as if I were just a thing. I cried out for my parents, who I looked up to, to help me, guide me, and love me. But my wish was never fulfilled. I cannot remember my father ever kissing me, wrestling with me, going for walks with me, or taking the time to help me overcome my fears and deal with my anxieties. The only attention I received from him was when I did something wrong.

The only time my father showed me any affection was when I saved his life. I was around eight at the time. After a violent argument, my mother ran out of the house and my father went into the kitchen, and I ran after him. Ignoring my pleas for some explanation of why my mother had fled, he turned on the gas stove and placed his head inside the oven. I could smell the gas, and I knew my father was doing something bad, because I had always been told never to turn on the gas stove. Desperate, I pulled on my father's shirt, pleading with him to turn off the gas, to pull his head out of the oven. "Please! Daddy," I cried out. "Don't do that, I love you, I need you." After what seemed like an eternity of tugging and tearful pleading, he heeded my pleas and hugged me. It was the first and last hug my father ever gave me.

It is important to point out that I don't consider my father a monster. He was a man of sterling integrity. He always paid his bills on time and had a deep respect for the truth and an appreciation for orderliness and cleanliness. During the Great Depression, he did whatever he could to make sure that his family wouldn't want for food, shelter, or clothing. I am convinced he did the best job he could to assure stability for his family.

However, he wasn't aware of why he would strike me, belittle me, and refuse my pleas for his attention, direction, and affection. Like me, he had abusive parents, especially his father. This became clear to me while digging into my past. I recalled the time when my father shared a childhood experience he had had while in his native Russia.

It was early spring, cold enough, he thought, to skate on the lake near his father's farm. When he fell through the ice, he was afraid to go home. He knew that if his father saw him drenched he would be whipped. So he spent the night in the barn, shivering, getting little sleep. When he sensed that his father had left the house in the morning, he slipped in. In a few days he was fighting for his life, sick with pneumonia.

We now know that a parent who has been abused as a child will in turn most likely abuse his or her own children. The safeguard against carrying out what your abusive parents modeled during your childhood is to make an earnest exploration of how and why you developed your false self. The understanding you will gain from such an undertaking will create a personal warning system that usually kicks in whenever there is an inclination to abuse.

I can truly say that connecting with my family's behavioral history helped me discover how my false self developed and what happened to my true self in the process. As a result of my breakthrough, I now understand why I hungered so much for respect from my peers and from those who wielded power: I yearned for the respect my father never gave me. It became clear why I bristled whenever I was criticized: It was a reminder of my father's name-calling. I now understand why I would grow defensive whenever I was accused of making a mistake or being wrong: It revived the pain generated by my father's incessant fault finding.

As my hidden past unraveled, I discovered that I had been spiritually abused as well as physically and emotionally abused. As a small child, I found the concept of God too abstract to fathom. My father was my god. To me he was superhuman and could do no wrong. So when my god hit me, belittled me, and found fault with me, I grew more and more insecure and sad that the god I loved so much didn't love me. This was a form of spiritual abuse.

I can now understand why as a teenager I rebelled against my god and rejection the notion of a higher power. My only experience with a higher power had been a terrible disappointment, a deeply painful experience. Because I could not trust anyone but myself, I turned myself into a god and developed an "I know best" attitude. I rejected religion as an impediment to human progress, and I didn't want anything to do with anyone who was religious.

Yet today I am a religious person. What led to this change of heart? Two fellow college students came to my rescue during a low point in my life. Their compassion moved me. They took the time to listen to my concerns and fears wholeheartedly, with a sincerity I had never experienced before. I sensed that they truly cared, and as a result I shared feelings I had hidden from others. I was getting from them what I had always longed for—respect from someone who really cared about me.

We became friends, even though we had little in common. They were scholars and members of the Bahá'í Faith, and I was pursuing a career in baseball. Yet I needed to be with them because I felt good in their presence. At the time I didn't know why I felt that way. Years later, after embracing the Bahá'í Faith, I realized what that good feeling was: I was discovering the spiritual aspect of my nature. My soul was a awakening.

Fortunately, my friends never told me what was happening to me. Had they tried, I would have severed our friendship, because I wasn't ready to deal with spirituality on an intellectual level at that time. I shall forever be grateful for their patience and wisdom.

Now that I understand why I created a false self and how it manifested itself, I feel more complete as a human being. The poison of my past, which festered within me for decades, is being released. Today I am able to forgive the hurts of the past. Now can I feel the thrill of the heart-purifying expression of forgiveness. I have forgiven my real and imagined enemies.

Though my father, too, had difficulty forgiving, I believe he forgave me shortly before he died. He never said so directly. The message was conveyed through an emotion he expressed when I visited him in a New Jersey nursing home where he was convalescing from a stroke that had immobilized him and left him speechless. I'll never forget that moment, and I sense it is locked in my father's soul as well.

An orderly wheeled my father into the lounge where my eldest son and I were waiting. It wasn't easy sitting there, wondering how I would be greeted. Though I tried to block out the past, I evidently didn't do a good job, for the pain of my childhood seized me. Even though my father was feeble, no longer able to strike me, a sense of fear swept over me. So did the guilt of trying to avoid my father during my adult years. When the orderly left, I moved my chair next to my father's wheelchair and ran my fingers over his forehead. It was my way of telling him I loved him. I was incapable of communicating it any other way.

The fear in his eyes disturbed me. I didn't know whether being in my presence had set off that emotion, whether he sensed his impending death, or whether it was a cry for help. I didn't know what to say for fear of making him more uncomfortable. But I knew I couldn't sit there without saying anything, for it might be the last time I would see him. What came from my mouth was something I hadn't planned. I shared with my father an experience I had two years earlier. Since he was Jewish, I sensed he would want to hear about it. It was one of the most memorable experiences of my life.

As I described my pilgrimage to the Holy Land, I sensed his fear disappearing. When I described how I had felt as the plane landed in Israel, my father began to cry. I had never seen him do this before. Without thinking, I embraced him and, crying myself, said, "I love you, Daddy."

Two months later my father passed away.

THINGS YOU CAN DO:

1. Take a step back, detach yourself, and consult with others you trust about your life. Form a support group with others like yourself who are trying to discover their true

self. If necessary, confront your past, perhaps with the help of a therapist. Be prepared for pain. A conscientious struggle requires it. A year in group therapy proved helpful for me.

2. Forgive yourself, forgive those you love, and forgive others around you, including those who have wronged you. When we do this, we become liberated.

3. Don't waste your precious time holding back your feelings and emotions. If someone does something that moves you, tell them.

15

Perfecting the Communications System Called Prayer

By dismantling my false self and developing my true self, I became able to use the God-given tools for spiritual development more effectively. Prayer is one of those tools. Unfortunately, not everyone who prays has the same understanding of what the act is. Many do it because their parents did it. Others do it for fear of spending an eternity burning in hell. And others, who have rejected religion as irrelevant, view prayer as a meaningless psychological crutch. The pragmatist uses it as a device to assure effective survival in an uncertain society, willing to try anything that has a record of generating some success in obtaining what they want. Others use prayer as a means of separating themselves from those they consider unholy and sinful. It seems that the more ardently they pray, the more they distance themselves from those who don't share their religious views.

To some people, prayer is like pressing a vending-machine button to obtain a product. It is true that in prayer we often beseech and ask, and that could be construed figuratively as pushing a button, albeit a spiritual button. But unlike purchasing a soft drink from a vending machine, when we pray we shouldn't try to anticipate God's response. Unfortunately, such attitudes toward prayer are a reflection of a spiritually disoriented and debased culture.

Prayer is a sacred rite that is absolutely essential to the spiritual development process. It is a ladder to the Kingdom of God, a God-given aid to help us discover, release, and develop our true self. Without prayer there is no way of gaining divine assistance; instead we are forced to rely on our physical nature to deal with all aspects of life, functioning as incomplete human beings, ignorant of the latent creative powers that only prayer can release. Only those who possess a healthy understanding of the reality of prayer can appreciate what those who don't resort to prayer are missing. To me, the height of ignorance and arrogance is for highly accomplished women and men to dismiss the practice of prayer without ever having seriously tried it themselves.

They even ignore scientific studies of the power of prayer. Many academics disregard the findings of legitimate studies on prayer because the findings seriously challenge their skepticism toward religion. They cling to their biases like babes clinging to the breast during weaning time. Dr. Larry Dossey, in his book *Healing Words*, cites compelling studies that prove prayer can be an instrument for good—that it works. How well, the studies show, depends on the one who prays. Motive and attitude are key factors. Prayers offered with a "Thy will be done" attitude produce the best results.

For the benefit of the purist in the scientific community, Dr. Dossey cites many studies that followed the scientific method, scrupulously avoiding any reliance on anecdotal evidence. For example, In a number of studies, prayer was employed to grow microorganisms. The microorganisms that were prayed for grew much faster and more abundantly than those that were ignored.[1] While studies like this haven't created much of a stir among researchers, some scientists have openly acknowledged the power of prayer. The late Alexis Carrel, a biologist and surgeon and 1912 Nobel Prize winner in Physiology or Medicine, viewed prayer as a potential instrument for healing. Dr. Carrel witnessed its power:

> The most important cases of miraculous healing have been recorded by the Medical Bureau of Lourdes. Our present conception of the influence of prayer upon pathological lesions is based upon the observation of patients who have been cured almost instantaneously of various afflictions. . . . The process of healing changes little from one individual to another. Often, an acute pain. Then a sudden sensation of being cured. In a few seconds, a few minutes, at the most a few hours, wounds are cicatrized, pathological symptoms disappear, appetite returns. Sometimes functional disorders vanish before the anatomical lesions are repaired. The skeletal deformations of Pott's disease, the cancerous glands, may still persist two or three days after the healing of the main lesions. The miracle is chiefly characterized by an extreme acceleration of the processes of organic repair. There is no doubt that the rate of cicatrization of the anatomical defects is much greater than the normal one. The only condition indispensable to the occurrences of the phenomenon is prayer. But there is no need for the patient himself to pray, or even to have any religious faith. It is sufficient that some one around him be in a state of prayer.[2]

Prayer is more than an appeal for help; it is an acknowledgment and appreciation of God's existence and supreme creative power. When offered sincerely, it is the most profound expression of love a human being can express. It is an act of surrender, of throwing ourselves at the threshold of our Creator's mercy. It is a sincere willingness to have God do what He wishes for us, our offering being based on the belief that whatever form the guidance takes is best for us.

Speaking as a Voice of God, Bahá'u'lláh shares with humanity what constitutes the process of prayer. To trigger the process, love is required: *"Love Me, that I may love thee. If thou lovest Me not, My love can in no wise reach thee. Know this, O, servant."*[3] This interchange of love has more to do with feeling than with words. Desire and trust are essential feelings to loving. Without trust there can be no genuine desire to share all. Isn't the fullest expression of love a willingness to share one's innermost thoughts and feelings with another?

If a carefully crafted prayer fails to spring from a sincere and loving heart, there can be no effective communication with the Divine. On the other hand, if crudely formed sentences flow from a pure heart, a divine response will be forthcoming. An Alaskan Tlingit Indian elder once told me that "the Creator never listens to our words, only to our heart."

Only God can judge who is sincere in prayer. But most of us experience obstacles that prevent us from attaining sincerity in our supplications. For example, it may be our enthusiasm to accomplish a crucial task that drives us to try to bargain with God, finding ourselves thinking something like this: "Oh, God! If you help me to secure this job promotion, I'll start going to church every Sunday." This is an act of willfulness that springs from the ego. By insisting that God fulfill our desire, we challenge His authority and question His wisdom. Usually when we resort to demanding that God do our bidding, we are demonstrating our lack of understanding of what our relationship with Him should be. But there are times when even though we are aware of God's station, we insist, out of desperation, that God carry out our wish. The order is usually issued when we witness, or are the target of, some great injustice. It is more like a child running to a parent with an appeal that action be taken to correct a wrong committed against himself or a friend.

Certainly God knows our motives, even our subconscious drives, which are not clear to us. What may be construed as a demand of God by someone may not be viewed that way by God at all. Of course, if we are headstrong and insist that God heed our wishes, then what we anticipate won't materialize. God will respond with what we really need, and that might come in the form of a challenge or two.

There is nothing wrong in asking God for something. But once the request is made, there is no need to push it. By doing that we limit God; we act as if He is hard of hearing or doesn't really understand what we want, when in fact He knows our thoughts before they are formulated. This doesn't mean that we shouldn't repeat our requests. What matters is how we make the request. The ideal attitude is to let go of the message we file with God and await His response, believing that whatever the response may be, it will be right.

Not all answers to prayer are as dramatic as the Kelsey family's discovery of a pot of cash in an open field. It may come by way of a phone call from a stranger or a friend who, during conversation, shares the information you are seeking. Someone you meet in the park or supermarket may be the vehicle by which the divine response comes to you. What is important is to believe that there will be an answer and to be on the lookout for it. A joke I heard a number of years ago best illustrates how God answers our prayers:

During the flooding of a town along the Mississippi River, all but one man fled their homes. The man stood on his roof with his arms stretched toward the sky. Shortly after calling on God to save him, a boat came by, and a policeman called out, "Do you need any help?" The man on the roof said, "No, God will provide the help I need." Moments later the man prayed again. It wasn't long before another boat appeared, asking the man if he needed help. Again he refused, declaring that God would come to his rescue. The rain intensified, and the house the man was standing on collapsed. Shortly afterward, he drowned. He soon found himself in heaven before God. Puzzled, the man said, "God, why didn't you come to my rescue when I begged for it?"

"I did answer your calls for help," said God. "But you rejected my help."

"How?"

"By refusing to board the boats I sent your way."

Praying isn't always easy, especially if we feel unworthy of communing with God because we feel guilty about some of the things we have done in the past. "He must be disappointed in me," we think—and fear facing Him. But God is All-Merciful and aware of our imperfections and the effort needed to progress spiritually, especially during these days when materialism pervades every aspect of life, including religion. To turn our backs on God because we feel unworthy of His help could put us in a tailspin toward destruction, intensifying our sense of guilt. We are human, and we are going to make mistakes. But the number of mistakes and indiscretions will diminish as we proceed along the pathway of spiritual growth. The more progress we make, the more capable we'll be in facing and learning from our tests. And eventually we'll realize that the greatest mistake is to stop relying on God no matter how severe life may seem, no matter how inadequate we feel, no matter how low we think we are spiritually. By continually reaching out to God, regardless of our situation or state of mind, our dependency on Him will grow, and we'll understand, as the wise ones do, that God is the first one to turn to.

Some of us want to turn to God but feel awkward in addressing Him, especially during times of great disappointment. To resort to prayer in the face of disappointment requires a belief that God answers prayers, an ability to discern the guidance He gives and to accept it, certain that it is right. Not everyone can do this, especially those of us who come from an atheistic or agnostic background. Even some who pray ardently have trouble. Undoubtedly, some have learned by experience through of trial and error, but there are also sincere souls who are unable to distinguish a divine sign from the multitude of events they are exposed to daily. For them, and for everyone else, there are various approaches to prayer, one of which was shared by Shoghi Effendi, the late Guardian of the Bahá'í Faith. He shared it with an American Bahá'í, Ruth Moffett, while she visiting the Bahá'í World Center in Haifa, Israel. He described five steps that could be taken when we approach God with a problem and wish for His help. I have paraphrased them here:

FIRST STEP—Pray and meditate about a problem or desire. Use the prayers of the divine educators, as they have the greatest power. Then remain in the silence of contemplation for a few minutes.

SECOND STEP—Arrive at a decision and hold this. This decision is usually born during the contemplation. It may seem to be impossible to accomplish, but if it seems to be an answer to a prayer or a way of solving a problem, then immediately take the next step.

THIRD STEP—Have determination to carry the decision through. Many fail here. The decision, budding into determination, is blighted and instead becomes a wish or a vague longing. When determination is born, immediately take the next step.

FOURTH STEP—Have faith and confidence that the power will flow through you, the right way will appear, the door will open, the right thought, the right message, the right principle, or the right book will be given to you. Have confidence, and the right thing will come to your need. Then, as you rise from prayer, take at once the fifth step.

FIFTH STEP—Then act; act as though it had all been answered. Then act with tireless, ceaseless energy. And as you act, you, yourself, will become a magnet, which will attract more power to your being, until you become an unobstructed channel for the Divine power to flow through you.[4]

Many pray but do not remain for the last half of the first step. Some who meditate arrive at the decision, but fail to hold it. Few have the determination to carry the decision through, and still fewer have the confidence that the right thing will come to their need. But how many remember to act as though it had all been answered? How true are the words "Greater than the prayer is the spirit in which it is uttered," and greater than the way it is uttered is the spirit in which it is carried out.

It is most important to integrate prayer into our daily schedule and to rely on it as we would food and drink. Prayer, though it is often terribly neglected, is a necessity of life.

We often associate prayer with a house of worship or a special place where we can be alone and commune with our Creator. But perhaps the highest form of prayer is the way we interact with our fellow human beings on all levels. Whatever we do is done prayerfully, with a consciousness of God's nearness and His desire to assist us in carrying out an important responsibility as well as a seemingly simple task. With such an awareness we will tackle everything we do with a constant call in our hearts for God's help. When an accountant, truck driver, police officer, or doctor approaches their work with such an attitude, good things will result. Coworkers will be attracted to them, will trust them, and will seek their advice. Others will be drawn to them because they will sense genuine love and a spirit of service. This kind of magnetism cannot be manufactured through human will. It results from a love of God that is constant and a willingness to become an open channel for His guidance. Fortunately, everyone has the capacity to manifest that kind of spirit.

THINGS YOU CAN DO:

1. Try an experiment. Focus on God through one of the divine educators; express your love for God. Remember, it isn't what you say but how you express yourself that is important. Then think. Sit down by yourself in a quiet place and think about something that concerns you. Say a prayer, whether it is in your own words or the words of Jesus, Buddha, Moses, Muḥammad, or Bahá'u'lláh. Reflect for a moment or two. It is highly likely that your mind will focus on a possible solution. Act on that solution. Go on with your day, confident in the absolute knowledge that it is correct, then wait and see what happens.

2. Remember to strive to develop a prayerful attitude. Every thought that springs from love for God is a prayer. When we view every thought as a prayer, we become more positive in our outlook despite the hardships we must face. When we engage in such thinking we become more positive and assured because we are certain of God's assistance in whatever we do, whatever condition we are in. In a sense, we find security in a divine sanctuary. That sanctuary is our awareness of our connection to God.

16

Internalizing the Word of God

There is more to the spiritual development process than prayer. Deepening our knowledge and understanding of the revealed Word of God is also required. The difference between prayer and deepening is that when we pray we are appealing to God; when we deepen we are trying to internalize God's guidance for our lives. The guidance, which has been revealed by divine educators, constitutes a spiritual map that can show us the way to reach the essential destinations in our spiritual journey called life.

While deepening and prayer are different, they are closely associated. In fact, deepening is most effective when we approach the task with a prayerful attitude. Assuming a prayerful attitude when we deepen safeguards us against vainglory and helps us acquire humility. Continually beseeching the assistance of a loving God produces a humble attitude in the person who is praying.

As we study the writings of the divine educators, it behooves us to call upon God for help in understanding what we are pondering. Such a call springs from a pure heart. To help us assume an appropriate attitude, listening to meditative music can be helpful. So is prayer before beginning the deepening.

The prayer I often recite before immersing myself in divinely revealed teachings provides me with a wholesome spiritual focus:

O God! Refresh and gladden my spirit. Purify my heart. Illumine my powers. I lay all my affairs in Thy hand. Thou art my Guide and Refuge. I will no longer be sorrowful and grieved; I will be a happy and joyful being. O God! I will no longer be full of anxiety, nor will I let trouble harass me. I will not dwell on the unpleasant things of life.

O God! Thou art more friend to me than I am to myself. I dedicate myself to Thee, O Lord.[1]

After the prayer, I engage in a deep-breathing exercise for a few minutes, focusing only on my breathing. In a matter of moments, my body and mind are united. I am at peace, and any thoughts of the past, present, or future have faded away. I am focused on the here and now, an empty receptacle, ready to penetrate and absorb the sacred writings before me.

With the love of God embedded in our consciousness, exploring the Word of God becomes a thrilling adventure; we look forward to what we will find. In a way, we are like miners working a vein of gold. Digging for the precious object becomes a joy because of the anticipation of what is in store at the end of the project.

Deepening can also be likened to recharging a battery. If we deepen daily, our spiritual energy grows. When that happens, we see the necessity for involvement in the spiritual development process; we develop a desire to do good deeds and gain a real appreciation for deepening as the mainspring of spiritual energy. As we continue the process of deepening, it will become apparent to us how important it is to include deepening in our daily routine. We learn from experience, having felt the power that springs from the Word of God surging in our hearts, making us more alert, more conscious of others' needs and concerns, more kindly, more loving, more desirous of wanting to help others. To be cut off from that power becomes our greatest fear.

Deepening is not a complicated process. It's a little bit like growing a flower. With the proper amount of water, sunlight, and cultivation, the seed grows and eventually blossoms. In a sense, reading from the Word of God and meditating on what we read are to us as water and sunlight are to a plant. Without essential care, the flower wilts. Without partaking of the soul-enriching water found in the divine verses, we shrivel up spiritually.

The term "deepening" implies immersion. We are like a perspiring man standing on the shore of a cool lake at high noon on a blistering hot day, seeking relief. He is aware of the body of water, but he cannot fully appreciate it until he plunges into it. The divine educators invite us to plunge into their revelations, knowing how much it will benefit us. Bahá'u'lláh, for example, writes, *"Immerse yourselves in the ocean of My words, that ye may unravel its secrets, and discover all the pearls of wisdom that lie hid in its depths."*[2]

To be engaged in true deepening, we need to understand as well as to know the Word of God. It is possible to know a great deal and understand very little. For example, had the man on the lakeshore refused to enter the water, he might have been able to describe the size, shape, and color of the lake, but he wouldn't have been able to describe how it felt.

Understanding generates feelings of enthusiasm, wonderment, and security. These are the emotions we equate with discovery. If we are not experiencing them, our spiritual growth

is stunted. There is a distinction between knowing and understanding, which often eludes us. Understanding is more than
knowing, though we cannot understand if we do not first know.
How do we gain understanding? One way—and perhaps the
most significant way—is by meditating on what we read.

In essence, meditating on the Holy Writings is reflective
reading, or spiritual daydreaming. We read, and then we stop
to ponder what we have read. This pondering can produce
exciting results. Meaningful insight or understanding of a
passage comes like a light breaking through dark clouds. The
elation that accompanies this discovery makes us yearn to
put into practice what we have discovered, and then we take
action. Where there is understanding, there is a genuine desire to carry it out in action. Simply knowing doesn't spark
action. This is an important distinction.

For example, there are many people who know that racism is an ugly, destructive social force, but they do nothing
to eradicate it within themselves or in the society in which
they live. Their knowledge of racism comes from reading
about it or from radio or television. When they are confronted
by it in the media, they may express sincere concern, but
eventually they turn their attention to other matters they
feel are more important. Through meditation, however, we
can gain an appreciation of the destructiveness of racism,
because we will think deeply about it, sometimes so deeply
that we sense the frustration and inner pain the victims of
racism endure. Action usually follows such an experience
because it arouses us emotionally, and we want to do something to help. Perhaps the first step is to inquire more about

racism so that meaningful measures can be taken to solve the problem. Because meditation reveals so much to us, we employ it again and again, and through it our understanding of racism continues to grow deeper and deeper.

Imagine what can happen to us if, through meditation, we continue to gain understanding of the Word of God. We will gain greater insight into our true self and will, as a consequence, grow more detached, dwelling more and more in the world of the spirit. We will become spiritually rooted and will learn routinely to draw upon spiritual energy to solve everyday problems.

Really, all that deepening involves is reading with thoughtful care. Whether we experience brilliant flashes of insight or find that understanding comes to us through slow and methodical meditation is of no consequence. What matters most is the effort we make to reflect on the Word of God. As long as we make the effort, understanding will eventually come, though not always when we expect it. We may read and meditate on a passage in the morning, and while driving home from work perhaps a new understanding of that passage unfolds in our mind. Whatever tensions we have accumulated during the day vanish, and joy overcomes us.

Sometimes, however, when our minds aren't riddled with family and work problems, when our spirit is truly refreshed, understanding comes quickly, at times during meditation itself. For most of us that doesn't happen often, mainly because we don't always approach deepening with a clear mind. A child may be sick, there may be unpaid bills, and perhaps there are five other things that need our immediate attention. So enlightenment doesn't necessarily come when we deepen. Yet there's no need to fret, because there will be times when understanding does come.

Eventually—if we are faithful in deepening regularly— we'll find a way to clear our minds, and we'll gain understanding more often. But even when we reach this stage in our spiritual development, there's no guarantee that enlightenment will come every time we deepen. It's not an automatic process even though we want it to be. Nonetheless, the effort is worth the result, because gaining new understanding fuels the fire of the love of God in our hearts. It gives us more vitality and reinforces our developing spiritual armor, which protects us from the assaults of the world around us.

Some of us may feel that deepening works for other people who are spiritually developed but not for us. We want to do it, but we resist doing it. We don't talk about this with others, because our resistance is a personal matter. Often it has to do with our spiritual condition. Perhaps things we have done that we regret or feel ashamed of are still plaguing us. To try to deepen, we feel, would be hypocritical. So we find ourselves in a tug-of-war: Guilt and unworthiness pull us in one direction, and the Creative Force pulls us toward itself. If this is how we are feeling, we need to deepen to become worthy. What we did in the past has shaped our attitudes and behavior, but we can change by examining ourselves and by delving into the Word of God on a regular basis. Deepening and prayer provide us with the encouragement and inspiration to seek the cause of troubled behavior and replace it with more spiritual behavior.

But sometimes even our awareness of the power of the Word of God to transform our lives doesn't move us to deepen regularly. Perhaps we are prevented by a deep-rooted problem stemming from a lifelong indoctrination that we are fundamentally evil. Perhaps we were taught to believe that human beings are born as sinners and are fundamentally bad. Perhaps we believe that we are bad until we prove ourselves good, or until we have accomplished something that society defines as good. Even atheists and agnostics brought up in Christian homes have adopted this attitude despite their conscious rejection of doctrine of original sin. They have been affected by this attitude, because they grew up in a culture that was shaped, in large measure, by the dominant religion, which preaches original sin. This attitude has unconsciously seeped into our psyche. Intellectually, many of us accept the idea that humans are born potentially good. How refreshing, we think. But deep down we have difficulty accepting the idea because it conflicts with what society tells us.

To allow the idea of original sin to paralyze us spiritually is like being unjustly sentenced to life imprisonment. Through deepening and prayer, which are independent of man-made religious dogma, we can win our spiritual freedom. The transformation that takes place through deepening and prayer requires steady effort. At first, not much change is noticeable, and that may prove discouraging for those who are impatient and want immediate positive results.

Most of us want to change for the better, to rid ourselves of character defects. If we have tried to will those flaws away and failed, we may be reluctant to try again, because failure is painful and can undermine our confidence. Without support from our Higher Power, we may end up flagellating ourselves psychologically. To avoid feeling sorry for ourselves, we may adopt a superior attitude toward others, becoming self-righteous and critical of those who aren't achieving what we think we have achieved in terms of character development. If this is our attitude, to be good becomes an emotional strain. In some cases, the strain may become so intense that we break down, ending our program of personal development and reverting to some of the very character flaws we were trying to eliminate.

But if we seek God's assistance through prayer and deepening, the changes we try to make in ourselves will be far more powerful than if we rely solely on human will. For those who are experiencing spiritual growth, personal transformation happens differently. It is like being involved in a process where growth and shedding occur simultaneously. As we grow in our understanding of our true self and the Creative Word, we become able to shed our flaws, and our false self begins to disintegrate.

I am sure many devout believers of all faiths have experienced this phenomenon. As a Bahá'í, however, I am most familiar with the struggles of some of my fellow believers. My young friend Bob's experience is a dramatic example.

Though Bob was touched by the message of Bahá'u'lláh and had just become a Bahá'í, his propensity for lying didn't automatically vanish. He had to train himself to be honest. His commitment to heed the divine educators' appeal to "know thyself" helped him considerably. Through his struggle to discover his true self, he learned why lying had become for him a perfectly natural means of protecting pretenses that he had conditioned himself to believe were aspects of his reality. It had also become a useful tool during times of crisis.

Bob had always lied because his parents lied, as did their parents. Lying was a natural part of their lives because it was a useful means of surviving in a hostile society. So lying had been ingrained in him as a child.

Bob couldn't be kept out of his new religion because of a character flaw, for if that were the case, then most of his fellow believers would have been barred from membership too. Yet he knew he had a responsibility to overcome this character flaw. The responsibility became a commitment when he read in the Bahá'í writings, *"Truthfulness is the foundation of all human virtues."* [3]

He knew that it would be a tough job because knowing something intellectually is one thing, but changing a lifelong behavior is another thing. Fortunately, by becoming spiritually oriented, Bob acquired some tools to make the changeover. But that was no guarantee that the effort would be painless, and it wasn't.

He began to deepen and pray, making time in the morning before going to work and making time in the evening before going to bed. He even bought an alarm clock to make sure he got up thirty minutes before his usual time. A week after he started his program of prayer and deepening he was tested at work. His foreman asked a question and he lied, just as he always had, without hesitation. But when the foreman left, he realized that he had lied, and this was something he would never have concerned himself with in the past. His new awareness was a sign of progress toward overcoming the character flaw, and it signified the development of the young man's conscience.

A month later—still deepening and praying every day—Bob was tested again. This time he hesitated before answering a coworker, wondering if he should tell the truth or lie. He succumbed to the pull of the past and lied, and for a few minutes he felt guilty about not having the strength to overcome his natural inclination. Though he had lied again, the young man was making progress.

He continued to deepen and pray regularly. Three weeks later, he was faced with another test. He lied again, but this time, before he uttered a word, his chest and throat tightened and he couldn't look at the person he had lied to. Afterward he berated himself for more than an hour for not telling the truth. Obviously, he was making more progress.

Three months went by. Still faithfully praying and deepening, he was confronted by a former friend about a matter that had taken place long before he made his commitment not to lie. He wished he could disappear. The friend sensed his uneasiness and wondered if Bob was ill. In a way he was, for the thought of lying made him nauseous—but he lied anyway. For the remainder of the day he was conscience-stricken, and he even had difficulty sleeping that night.

After a year of praying and deepening, a process he had learned to enjoy and now wouldn't think of missing, Bob was tested again. This time he was seized with pain in his chest and began to sweat. He hesitated so long that the person he was talking to asked the question a second time. In torment, he sat down and placed his head in his hands. He wanted desperately to tell the truth, yet he felt the tug of the past.

Suddenly, he opened his eyes, looked at the foreman who was standing over him, and told him the truth. The pain in his chest disappeared. There was a glow in his eyes. He felt like dancing. The foreman, meanwhile, was perplexed, wondering if the young man was on some sort of narcotic. He had never seen him so happy. This was a victory that only the young man could appreciate, a feeling of liberation he had never before experienced. He was not the same person he had been before starting his program of spiritual development. Could he ever go back to the way he was? Never! But this new awareness had not emerged instantly. He had always had the potential to be what he was now, but by deepening and praying regularly, he had nurtured and cultivated the seed of happiness within him.

Part of Bob's new understanding was a belief in the process of deepening and prayer. It would be foolish to abandon it, he felt, because doing that would be like ceasing to water a rosebush when it produced its first blossom. To stop would be to commit spiritual suicide. He knew that it was a process in which he would be engaged for the rest of his life, for he was far from being a saint. Because he experienced the benefits of the process, he made a lifelong commitment to it and looked forward to the guidance he knew he would receive, the growth he would experience, the insights he would gain.

One of the insights that thrilled him most was discovering his innate nobility. He read from Bahá'u'lláh's writings:

O Son of Spirit!
I created thee rich, why dost thou bring thyself down to poverty? Noble I made thee, wherewith dost thou abase

thyself? Out of the essence of knowledge I gave thee being, why seekest thou enlightenment from anyone beside
Me? Out of the clay of love I molded thee, how dost thou
busy thyself with another? Turn thy sight unto thyself,
that thou mayest find Me standing within thee, mighty,
powerful and self-subsisting.[4]

THINGS YOU CAN DO:

1. Before deepening, get into a prayerful mood by going
to the place where you normally pray and deepen. Sit
quietly and meditate. Deepening with a prayerful attitude
usually produces the most meaningful insights.

2. Pray and deepen every day, even when you don't feel
like it. Taking such action will most likely help you overcome the inertia or resistance you feel toward praying and
deepening, putting you in a brighter mood and providing
you with the strength to meet life's never-ending challenges. Think of prayer and deepening as your spiritual
armor.

17

Finding Focus in Our Lives

Prayer and deepening are not the only spiritual development tools available to us. Taking oneself into account daily is yet another. This assessment can help to purify one's heart because it provides a means for understanding why we behave the way we do and why we repeat the same mistake time and time again. It's a way of keeping oneself on the spiritual path blazed by the divine educators. Taking oneself into account daily helps us focus on the true self, thereby gaining the knowledge and determination to dismantle the false self. It hastens the integration of our conscious and unconscious realities, which makes us whole. It can also help to keep us from becoming ridden with anxiety.

Taking oneself to account can be thought of as another form of meditation. It is an evaluation system: As we review our day's activities, we evaluate the good done, the missed opportunities to do good, the mistakes made, insensitive acts and statements, and immoral thoughts and actions. For maximum results it is helpful if we approach the exercise in a prayerful condition, mindful that God is watching as a loving parent. This can serve as a safeguard against slipping into rationalization and accepting the excuses for our negative actions. It also helps to preserve our spiritual focus. For example, in reviewing the good we have done, we can express our gratitude to our Higher Power instead of inflating our ego. It is important that we give attention to the good we have done as well as to the mistakes and negative things not only because it is just and fair, but because it is a way of freeing ourselves from feelings of failure. Taking ourselves into account should not be an exercise in religious self-flagellation. We are potentially good, created noble, and we need to remind ourselves of this reality even as come to grips with our shortcomings. There are times when sensing that we are faltering spiritually will create in us a resolve never to make the same mistake again. Knowledge of God's guidelines for living is also helpful in the process of taking oneself into account. They provide a set of spiritual standards against which we can measure our daily actions and attitudes. They enable us to gauge our development, providing us with some idea of how far we must go to internalize a certain spiritual principle. This is why deepening is so important. The better we understand God's guidance for our lives, the greater the opportunity we have to grow spiritually.

I find that shortly before bedtime is the best time for me to take myself into account. It is usually quiet, all human interactions have been completed, and the likelihood of interruptions is minimal. This is when I can give the process my fullest attention.

When an unresolved problem relevant to an activity that day pops into my consciousness during the exercise, I don't set it aside until I have gone through a mental checklist. If I set it aside, the problem will probably slip out of my consciousness, and I would lose the opportunity to find a solution. During this private problem-solving session there are usually plenty of opportunities to evaluate my actions and attitudes in dealing with the problem up to that point. I find it is important to make a thorough check of my motives, because by checking routinely the practice that has become a natural reflex throughout the day in all of my dealings. It is another way of strengthening my conscience and staying focused on my true self.

By taking oneself into account daily, we can better understand the persona we manifest in public. If we are sincere and honest in our self-evaluations, we become aware of our shortcomings and character weaknesses. Gaining self-knowledge is the first step toward emotional and spiritual health, and it takes courage and steadfastness to face what we discover. Dealing with our shortcomings and character weaknesses will most likely take us out of our comfort zone and give rise to fears we would prefer not to confront.

When such fear arose in me, I nearly panicked. Fortunately, I remembered who my "guide and refuge" is in this world and the next. I don't think I could have accepted what I discovered during the years I have been taking myself into account if it weren't for God's helping hand propping me up when my natural inclination was to fall back into the comfort of denial or rationalization.

My prayers not only provide me with the fortitude to accept what I uncover about myself, but also I am certain the format I devised to overcome my character flaws and destructive tendencies result from reaching out for God's help. With an awareness of some of my shortcomings, I have grown more acutely aware of what virtues need greater development. As a result, my personal prayer includes a call for their growth.

Interestingly, the list of my shortcomings and weaknesses has grown over the years. That is what happens when you continue to probe into your past and you grow more honest with yourself. I have found that because this process makes me freer, and I like that feeling, I no longer fear what I will discover. Knowing there is a way to overcoming the weakness builds confidence.

A friend of mine named Judy has benefited from the process. She says, "The neat thing about looking at the 'dark side' is that, however frightening it may be, it loses its power when exposed to the light. That was a well-kept secret for me until recently."

I have worked hard to overcome some of the weaknesses on my list, but I feel it isn't for me to judge my success. While I have noticed some of my character flaws fading, and in fact, I think some seem to have vanished, I haven't scratched them from the list. I just alter my message to God. Instead of praying, "Please help me to be patient," I now pray, "Thank you for giving me the patience I never had, and please keep me from losing it." I have resorted to this approach in order to prevent myself from becoming overconfident. Only God can be my judge as I struggle to grow spiritually.

While I form my list when I am taking myself into account at night, I address every item on it during my morning prayer and deepening period. This seems to be a good time for it because it is the beginning of my day, a time when I must put myself into spiritual gear to deal with the tests and difficulties of living in a materialistic society. In a way, it is like putting on spiritual armor. Bahá'u'lláh has written, "Armed with the power of Thy name nothing can ever hurt me, and with Thy love in my heart all the world's afflictions can in no wise alarm me."[1]

After deepening on the Word of God and reciting prayers revealed by a divine educator, I go through the list, which is a series of personal prayers in the form of heartfelt calls to God through the divine educator I am most familiar with. For the first year or so, this was the format I used:

Oh Bahá'u'lláh, please help me to be a good, kind, caring, loving, compassionate, and generous person. Help me to be truthful and honest. Help me to be humble and patient. Help me to be detached from the contingent world. Oh, help me to have a pure heart and open mind.

Bahá'u'lláh, please help me to get rid of every trace of bitterness and negativity. Help me to get rid of every trace of anger, hatred, and hostility. Help me to get rid of every trace of envy and jealousy. Please help me to get rid of every trace of egotism and selfishness.

Bahá'u'lláh, please help me to get rid of every trace of racism, sexism, and prejudice within me. Help me to get rid of every desire to hurt those who have hurt me, and help me to get rid of every desire to be a big shot in my Faith.*

---

* This is a personal prayer created by me. It is not part of the collection of prayers revealed by the central figures of the Bahá'í Faith.

Part of the list is an appeal for a few favors: "Please help me to become a healer and an instrument for good today. And help me with my writing, for without it I cannot do what I feel I must do."

I have discovered that this personal prayer is like a training exercise. By repeating it daily, I have brought all that I ask for into my consciousness. As a result, whenever I feel an inclination toward being impatient or lying, a warning signal flashes within me, and I usually don't carry out the inclination. When that happens, I thank God, and a sense of relief sweeps over me, at times lifting me into a state of joy.

This doesn't mean that I never fail to pass a personal test. There are times when I cave in to the promptings of my false self. But because certain spiritual standards have gradually become ingrained in me through my personal daily prayer, I'm aware of what I have done, and I don't like the feeling that results. A sense of shame grips me. Fortunately, I no longer allow shame to paralyze me spiritually. After berating myself a little, I ask God for forgiveness and pray for the strength not to bend to the impulses that spring from my false self, and I pray for the wisdom to follow without hesitation the divine laws applicable to the day in which I live.

THINGS YOU CAN DO:

1. Take yourself into account at the place where you normally pray and deepen. To clear your mind, pray before engaging in the procedure. Then reflect on your day, checking out the good things you did or experienced as

well as the missed opportunities to do good, and those times when you failed.

2. Try to determine why you failed so you don't repeat the mistake.

3. Check the sacred writings for guidance on ways to avoid mis-takes made and on anything else that may be bothering you.

4. If you have difficulty remembering things, carry a small pad of paper or index cards with you, and write experiences down as they occur so that you can think about them whenever you take yourself into account.

18

Divine Laws as Preventive Medicine

When most people think of laws, they think of courts, lawyers, the police, or parliaments debating. Sensible men and women recognize the value of laws. Without them chaos would reign. Imagine what would happen if there were no traffic lights on the corner of New York's Times Square and Forty-Second Street. Laws help societies remain civil.

But man-made laws are subject to change. Enlightenment usually prompts social change. When the majority of America's federal legislators recognized in the 1960s that racial segregation laws were a violation of human rights, they replaced them with new laws that were supposed to guarantee equal treatment for all Americans.

In a democratic society, a constitution, which is a collection of sacred laws that becomes the legal foundation of a nation, is usually amended from time to time. Amendments reflect a collective change in attitude that is usually prompted by a new awareness of a particular crucial issue. For example, the nineteenth amendment of the United States Constitution, which gave American women the right to vote, was adopted in 1920, about 150 years after the constitution was officially adopted.

There are other laws, however, that humans can't discard, laws they didn't fashion, laws people have learned to respect, for they are natural laws. Gravity is an example. So are relativity and the universal laws of oneness and unity in diversity, which are aspects of reality that were only recently recognized by a growing number of scientists. Many people still have difficulty accepting that all of Creation is interrelated, that the universe is a dynamic web of interlocking relationships. Those who recognize the law of oneness can appreciate what would happen if it were suddenly and mysteriously repealed.

Just as there are societal laws and laws that govern the operation of the universe, there are also divine laws. Divine laws are meant to help humans understand their reality and develop it fully, as well as create loving, unified communities based on justice. They are laws from which morality springs and is fortified. Like the physical laws of the universe, divine laws don't result from legislative negotiations or compromises. They have been revealed throughout history by God to humanity through His divine educators. Take, for example, the law requiring our love of God in order to receive God's love, which is constantly pouring forth. If we obey that law, we attract divine guidance. But when we reject or ignore it, we cut ourselves off from divine guidance. Think of the human being as a receptacle. When we express our love of God, the lid opens and His love flows into us, filling us with a sense of joy that money can't buy.

Compliance with divine laws can protect humans from succumbing to the animal impulses that are associated with our physical nature. Of course, following the divine laws doesn't spring from desire alone. There are cases where we want to do the right thing but fail more times than we succeed. Conscientious involvement in the spiritual development process results in new behavior and helps us develop a deepening appreciation of divine laws; we gain an understanding of why they were revealed and how they can benefit us and our community. This awareness reinforces our love for our Creator and leads to an even greater appreciation for the divine laws.

Understanding and internalizing divine law today isn't easy, because the divine laws have been devalued by popular culture. Fulfilling one's personal desires is seen as a sign of success, and how that happens doesn't seem to matter much.

Marvin, like so many others raised in orthodox religious homes, decided to disregard the spiritual influence of his childhood and youth. While he was in college he decided to partake of all the sensual pleasures that were available, and there were many. "To hell with the consequences," he thought. "I'm going to get my kicks like everyone else." While having sex, smoking pot, and drinking beer whenever he wanted to was appealing, the hypocrisy he witnessed among some of the religious leaders in his hometown influenced his attitudes. As a teenager he had been aware of the affair a clergyman was having with a local waitress, and he knew of the drinking problem several others had.

When Marvin married, he dropped out of the "anything goes" school of thought. He continued to drink beer once in a while or sip a few martinis at business lunches, but he quit seeking new sexual experiences. It seems that his conscience would not allow him to engage in extramarital affairs. After an excruciating test of will, Marvin realized his conscience had been shaped in large measure by his early exposure to the Ten Commandments. *"Thou shalt not commit adultery"* (Exodus 20:14) provided the necessary mental brakes.

After four years of marriage, those brakes nearly failed him. Though he loved his wife, it seemed like he was going to crash into an affair with one of his business colleagues.

The first time he saw Monica, the company's new human resources manager, he was impressed with her physical beauty. His attraction to her was so strong that he tried to avoid her, but that wasn't possible because she was the only one who could handle the behavioral problems in his department. As manager of his department, he had to interact with Monica; and that meant being alone with her, even having lunch with her. The fact that she was attracted to him and didn't hide this fact in his presence, didn't help matters. She invited him to her apartment for dinner, and this was a test he barely passed.

After a while, Marvin concocted situations where the two had to be together. When he began to daydream about making love to Monica, he sensed he was about to fall off the edge. Marvin's obsession triggered pangs of guilt, for he loved his wife, who was pregnant with their first child. The mere idea of her learning that he was having an affair with another woman was too painful to endure. Yet he couldn't get Monica out of his mind.

Marvin fell off the edge—once. He and Monica had a liaison at a motel. Though he wanted badly to continue the relationship, he realized he was in deep trouble and sought help from a pastoral counselor who had helped a close friend in a similar predicament.

It took some convincing on the part of the friend to get Marvin to see the counselor; Marvin felt uneasy about sharing his dilemma with a woman. But after the first session he sensed she could help him. It wasn't an overnight cure. After eighteen sessions, Marvin was able to extinguish his passion for Monica. Unlike the other clergy he had known as a youth, the pastoral counselor he consulted was able to provide him with a perspective that he could embrace. It was logical; it made sense.

The pastor wasn't afraid to share her own feelings about sex. She had strayed a number of times before marrying, once while studying at the seminary. As she grew spiritually, it became clear to her what the purpose of sex was. When she shared her insights with Marvin, he began to understand the divine laws regarding chastity before marriage and adultery. Though he couldn't recite what she said verbatim, he internalized the core of her views:

> I'm not opposed to sex; in fact, I enjoy it. It is both a sacred privilege and a duty reserved for married couples. It is a privilege because it can provide momentary pleasure; and it is a duty, because it is necessary for the procreation of the human race. I think the privilege and duty are intertwined. Without the privilege there would be no incentive to carry out the duty.
>
> Ideally, the sex act is an expression of love that is meant to strengthen the wife-husband relationship; it is a force for unity. However, when exercised outside of marriage, sex contributes to the kind of societal instability we experience today—and not only diseases, some of them fatal—it is also destroying the fabric that binds the family together. The disunified family is a dysfunctional family, and dysfunctional families lead to dysfunctional communities.
>
> The wife or husband is hurt by indiscriminate sex in many ways. There are usually feelings of guilt; the fear of

being caught and having to continually lie to prevent the spouse from finding out. And used as a vehicle for emotional release or as a means of conquest and dominance, sex, which is supposed to be a precious act, becomes a commonplace practice. It loses its spiritual value, becoming purely physical—like the daily run that sets off endorphin-induced highs.

THINGS YOU CAN DO:

1. Reflect on the divine laws you are aware of, and check out whether you are adhering to them. Remember, they were revealed for our benefit.

2. Look upon these laws as guidelines in meeting life's continuous challenges.

3. Think about the price we pay by ignoring these laws, not only on an individual basis, but on a community basis as well.

4. Daily prayer, deepening, and taking yourself into account each day strengthen your resolve to adhere to divine laws. Make time for them. They are essential to your spiritual progress. They are a form of spiritual sustenance that is as important as the daily intake of food and water.

STEP TEN *Spiritual Knowledge in Action*

STEP NINE *Preventive Medicine*

STEP EIGHT *Taking Yourself into Account*

STEP SEVEN *Deepening Our Understanding*

STEP SIX *Prayer*

STEP FIVE *Tools for Developing Our True Self*

STEP FOUR *Finding Our Spiritual Capacity*

STEP THREE *Religion & the Divine Educators*

STEP TWO *The Soul*

STEP ONE *Oneness*

19

The Purpose of Life

Freedom for an individual is becoming what we are meant to be. It has nothing to do with our career or where we live. You can be a ditchdigger or a prisoner and still be free. If we truly understand our spiritual nature and we are earnestly involved in fulfilling our purpose of life, we are experiencing true freedom.

Most of us have never seriously given much thought to our purpose in life. We take for granted the fact that we are human, much like a fish takes for granted the water in which he swims. Adapting to our environment and finding ways to live as comfortably as possible are probably our primary preoccupation.

But most of us, even the wealthy, sense something essential is missing from their lives. Fortunately, that something can be found when we learn our true purpose in life. No trip to a Tibetan monastery is necessary to find what we search for. Though what we seek is spiritual, most of us have not found it in churches or other religious institutions. To discover it, we must engage in a process of spiritual development.

The process is simple: There are three components to discovering our purpose in life. The first is to develop a conscious connection with our Higher Power. This is our spiritual lifeline, our umbilical cord. The strength of that connection is dependent upon the degree to which we know and love our Creator. The more we know and love God, the more we grow spiritually, which leads us to the second component—the development of the divine virtues latent within our souls. When both of those components are being nourished, the third component follows naturally—and that is active service to the world of humanity. Of course, this doesn't mean that must all become international altruists. We can each help to make the world a better place by improving the quality of life in our homes and neighborhoods, at work and at play. As you can see, all three components are intertwined.

Depending solely on human will has its limitations and can eventually lead to "burnout" and an unwillingness to continue. In contrast, drawing our energy from the force of the Almighty continually fortifies our desire to develop virtues and serve our community in a constructive way. The body of a highly spiritually developed person may grow tired, but the soul remains inspired to develop its powers and qualities and to fulfill its destiny. Since this soul is growing increasingly patient and compassionate, it can appreciate the need for the body to rest. But the reason for the rest and relaxation is to become more effective in developing virtues and helping to make the world a better place. To a highly spiritually developed person, there is no greater joy than this state of service.

Imagine a collective consciousness that is created and continually enriched by loving feelings, thoughts, opinions, and actions. It is possible, but it requires that the majority of people gain an understanding of their true selves and their purpose in this world. Without such an understanding, the problems that plague the world today will continue to worsen.

A simple thing like discovering one's true self—the soul—and engaging in a sustained effort to develop it will produce a more balanced human being who will naturally become a force for good and unity in the community in which she or he lives. When a critical mass of such individuals materializes, communities will be spiritually transformed from places of despair into centers of enlightenment.

It seems that our leaders do not understand that knowledge and development of the soul has any relevance to solving humanity's problems. It is too simplistic, they contend, and besides, they don't expect solutions from religion. How can you expect solutions from institutions that appear to be part of the problem? Many believe this but rarely express it in public because it would be politically incorrect to do so. As a consequence, our leaders continue to address the effects and not the cause of society's problems, which worsen with each passing day. Our leaders are like the physicians who can't stop the bleeding. Nothing they try really helps. Money is not the answer. Nor is the explosion of technological advancements. We seem to be searching in all directions except within ourselves, which is where the solution exists.

The first step toward peace and harmony within the individual, for the community, and the world, is for human beings to internalize the reality of the oneness of the human family.

The second step is to be aware of the soul's unique position within nature, realizing that each human being is a soul with a body and not a body with a soul. The soul is a spiritual emanation from God, and the relationship between God and human souls can be likened to the relationship between the sun and its rays. If we truly understand this truth, then our love for God will never wane, for we will realize that just as there cannot be any rays without the sun, there can be no humanity without God. With this understanding our love of God grows, and following His laws becomes a necessity.

The third step is to gain an understanding of religion's role in helping us define our spiritual capacity.

The fourth step is to find that spiritual capacity and commit ourselves to developing it.

The fifth step is to discover the divinely given tools that enable us to develop our spiritual capacity.

The sixth step is prayer.

The seventh step is deepening our knowledge and understanding of the Word of God so that we can internalize it.

The eighth step is to establish the daily practice of evaluating our spiritual development, which can provide focus in our lives.

The ninth step is to discover the divine laws that will enable us to avoid spiritual pitfalls. When we view them as preventative medicine, the divine laws become a potent means of avoiding setbacks. This step will also help us gain an understanding of the purpose of life.

The tenth step is to turn spiritual knowledge into action by being of service to the community around us.

While this ten-step program of spiritual development reflects some of the teachings of Bahá'u'lláh, it is not part of any official doctrine of the Bahá'í Faith. I created the program to assist readers and make the material more easily understood. It is important to note that the ten-step program is not a quick-fix spiritual solution. It represents a lifelong process that is designed to help us dismantle our false self and become more and more acquainted with our true self, thereby developing its latent powers and qualities.

To ensure positive results, remembering our relationship with our Creator is absolutely necessary. I am sure there are numerous reminders in the Christian, Jewish, and Muslim scriptures of this special relationship. The one I focus on was revealed by Bahá'u'lláh in the form of a daily obligatory prayer:

I bear witness, O my God, that Thou hast created me to know Thee and to worship Thee. I testify, at this moment, to my powerlessness and to Thy might, to my poverty and to Thy wealth.

There is none other God but Thee, the Help in Peril, the Self-Subsisting.[1]

20

Service to Our Fellow Human Beings

What can we gain from the ten-step program of spiritual development? We can gain an understanding of who we truly are as human beings, we can discover and understand our true self and our purpose of life, and we can gain the knowledge of how to develop our true self, the soul. Involvement in such a pursuit gives us an inner peace and strength and makes life, despite its ups and downs, a joyous and exciting adventure.

Engaging in a process of spiritual development also provides us with a new understanding of power. Real power, we learn, has nothing to do with physical strength, the ability to manipulate or dominate others, or amassing material wealth. In reality, power is the desire and the ability to serve others.

Mehdi was a powerful human being. Persecuted in his homeland of Iran, because he was a Bahá'í, he fled to America, leaving behind everything he owned, except the clothing on his back and a satchel full of books, which he considered his lifeline to sanity.

He partook of the freedoms and opportunities that his adopted land afforded him. In time, he became a highly respected professor at a medical school. While grateful to

America for the opportunity to pursue his profession and live in relative safety, he wasn't blind to certain negative aspects of the American way of life. One of the things that disturbed him most was the racism he observed. It wasn't directed against him, although during the First Gulf War he was once denounced as "a dirty Iraqi" by a shopper in his neighborhood supermarket.

Because his laboratory was located in a poor African-American section of the city, he became aware of the sense of helplessness and hopelessness that gripped most of the people who lived there. In many ways, the neighborhood reminded him of South Tehran, whose inhabitants believed it was their destiny to live in squalor and despair. As a young university student in Tehran, he had felt he should do something to help those people, and he did. Mehdi was able to persuade some college officials to allow him to teach in an elementary school where rats roamed freely in the unheated classroom, often snatching the children's lunch bags.

Mehdi spent two years as a volunteer teacher in the slums of Tehran while continuing his medical studies. Many of his friends thought he was crazy to do what he was doing. When he tried to explain to them that seeing hope replace despair in a child's face was a source of joy for him, they simply laughed and mocked him. Mehdi would have spent more than two years at that school, but he was ordered to leave it, "and never set foot on the premises again," by an irate, fanatical local Islamic cleric, who believed Bahá'ís were agents of Satan.

In America, Mehdi's desire to serve the downtrodden and oppressed was as vigorous as when he lived in Iran—perhaps even greater, because his understanding of the purpose of life was greater. He jumped at every opportunity to serve, especially those who were victims of social injustice. He was not driven by a desire to help his fellow family members. Mehdi believed that all human beings on the planet were members of his family. This belief was a reflection of his understanding of the oneness of humanity. Putting this belief into practice, he felt, was a way of expressing his love for God.

Troubled by the racism he observed in every area of his adopted land, he felt compelled to do something meaningful to eliminate it. To do nothing, he believed, would be unconscionable. Unaware of the gravity of the problem and how it originated and developed over the years, he vowed to educate himself. He read books and audited two Afro-American history classes. When he began to frequent some of the restaurants in the black neighborhood at night, some of his professional colleagues urged him to stop the habit; they feared for his life.

Grateful for their concern, he nevertheless continued to pursue his campaign to become acquainted with the problem of racism. To appreciate it, he needed to get to know black people and know them well enough so that they trusted him. Trust was necessary, he felt, in order to gain an appreciation of the depths of their wounds.

He made friends with a few men; one in particular stood out. Without Milton's help, Mehdi would not have been able to carry out his personal battle against racism. As a young minister fresh from the seminary, full of idealism and enthusiasm, Milton pledged to support Mehdi's effort to recruit black graduate students for his program and research project. In effect, Milton became Mehdi's recruiter.

Mehdi's plan called for providing an opportunity for African-Americans to earn PhDs in molecular genetic research. None had ever earned such a degree at his university. Furthermore, the faculty and administration doubted that it was possible. Though they never voiced it openly, most of them felt blacks were incapable of functioning effectively in the physical sciences. When the dean heard of Mehdi's idea, he tried to discourage him from implementing it, claiming that it could retard his research and eventually cut off his rather substantial source of government funding.

Fortunately, Mehdi's contract with the government stated that he had sole jurisdiction as to who would be accepted into his graduate program and assist in his research. Besides having their tuition paid for, the students would receive a $15,000 annual stipend.

Because of the cutting-edge research he was doing and the attractive financial package he was offering, Mehdi received about 250 applications for six openings. Most came from highly acclaimed graduates of the top American universities, and there were even a few from Oxford and Cambridge in Great Britain. Though none of those applicants were black, Milton found two who were. Roger was a graduate from an all-black college in the south; Hakim was a young man from the neighborhood where the medical school was located and a recent graduate of a state supported city college that was noted more for its basketball team than for its quality of scholarship.

When the dean discovered that Mehdi had accepted the two black applicants, who were statistically less qualified than the other applicants—in fact, one of them had done poorly on the National General Research Exam—he became irate, unable to withhold his displeasure. In a matter of days, the school was rife with rumor, and Mehdi became the brunt of fellow faculty jokes. The most popular one was that Mehdi was now heading the "remedial research department." While being the target of persistent backbiting was painful, Mehdi's commitment to carry out his antiracism campaign never wavered. It pained him to know that Roger and Hakim were aware of the rumors and backbiting. Both Mehdi and Milton spent hours with the two young men, shoring them up, assuring them that they could make it.

Hakim had the most doubts. Though he had taken the proper courses in college, he had not been exposed to the kind of academic rigor that was required of a physical science research program like Mehdi's.

Mehdi believed that Hakim could succeed in his program because the young man had a genuine interest in genetics and the kind of intuition that is needed for scientific breakthrough. As a consequence, Mehdi personally helped Hakim build up his physical science basics. At times he invited the young man to his suburban home, where the two would work all weekend on some of the things Hakim should have learned in college.

Mehdi's own intuition proved correct. After a yearlong struggle to keep pace with his Ivy League peers, Hakim, in the next three years, evolved into an academic star. Everything Mehdi sensed in the young man was realized.

In his third year, while assisting his professor, Hakim was struck by an idea that would require a separate course of investigation. When Mehdi learned about it, he encouraged

Hakim to pursue it, providing him with the facilities and funding to carry out his experiments.

It wasn't long before Hakim startled everyone in the department with a scientific breakthrough that became the source of his PhD dissertation. When news of Hakim's success reached the dean, the university's news bureau dispatched a reporter and photographer to Mehdi's laboratory to do interviews with the professor and his star pupil. A few days later the local media asked for interviews. A picture of the dean with Mehdi and Hakim was circulated to the public through the university's news bureau.

With Hakim earning celebrity status, the backbiting directed at Mehdi ceased. And no one, including the dean, ever again questioned his unorthodox admissions policy, which called for the admittance of two or three black students into his program every year.

In order to assure a continuing flow of graduate students into Mehdi's program, Milton launched a campaign to find high school seniors who demonstrated a sincere interest in biomedical sciences and followed them closely through their college years, then guided them into Mehdi's program.

Milton made sure that what Mehdi had done didn't escape the notice of the local black community. He organized a banquet in Mehdi's honor, where Hakim was the featured speaker. During his address, Hakim turned to Mehdi, who was at the same table, and said, "I have never had a teacher who cared for me the way Mehdi did. He made it possible for me to learn to believe in myself. Without that, I wouldn't have made it."

During Hakim's remarks, Mehdi thanked God for allowing him to serve his student. People like Mehdi—and there
aren't many of them around—won't take credit for their
achievements, because they view themselves as conduits of
God's will. Their greatest pleasure comes from functioning
in that capacity. Mehdi's attitude does not reflect any sense
of self-loathing. On the contrary, he loves himself. But that
love isn't based on a belief that he is superior to others; it is
based on his understanding of an important aspect of reality—his connection to God. He knows that if he dislikes
himself, he dislikes God. Mehdi loves God. He knows that
as a soul, he is a spiritual emanation of God. As he grows
spiritually, his tie to his Creator strengthens and he gains
more and more access to the limitless reservoir of knowledge
and love that is God. He taps into it as a means of solving
problems and meeting life's challenges.

Mehdi knows what a natural high is like.

THINGS YOU CAN DO:

1. Continually review the three phases of the purpose of
life in a detached manner, for they provide us with a focus
for our life's journey. They are to know and to love God, to
develop the virtues latent within the soul, and to help
make the world a better place.

2. When taking yourself into account, you will discover
talents and abilities. Think about how you can use these
talents and abilities to serve those close to you as well as
the community at large.

3. Don't be afraid! If you serve others for the sake of God, you will gain the courage to carry out what your heart prompts you to do.

4. Remember, when doing good deeds you will experience a sense of well-being.

5. Love and encourage others at all times. This is so important, because what we do in relation to those around us, whether it be holding a door open for someone or visiting a sick friend, has a ripple effect. If you make someone else feel good, they will spread that good feeling to others, and so on.

21

Accepting the Challenge

Getting others to focus on their spiritual development isn't easy. I'm sure we can all think of many sound reasons why most people will resist making the kind of commitment that is necessary to create healthier and happier individuals and communities. Most people are blind to the opportunities the process of spiritual growth presents. But when we consider the alternative to spiritual growth and transformation, I don't think we have much of a choice. If we reflect openly and honestly on humanity's present-day condition, we can't help but realize that we are on a course leading to greater travail and sorrow.

The most pressing challenge, therefore, is to break out of the trap and find the spiritual course that God has always intended for humanity to follow. Humanity has gotten sidetracked by distorted concepts of reality, but allowing ourselves to remain sidetracked will only bring greater grief and suffering.

We cannot wait for our leaders to direct the way, because they do not know the way. They owe their positions of leadership to the practices and traditions that, to a great extent, have created the perilous condition in which we find ourselves today. They are unwitting keepers of the trap, prisoners of a paradigm that is incapable of meeting the needs of the new age that humanity has entered. In fact, they themselves are in the trap and do not even know it.

Sadly, those leaders who are inclined to try new ways of solving chronic social problems meet such intense resistance that they usually give up for fear of losing their coveted positions. Those who insist on promoting unorthodox ideas are either branded as radicals and troublemakers or have to go underground to promote their campaigns and eventually fade into obscurity. Some are even martyred. The established systems do not allow for innovation based on rules outside the existing paradigm. This doesn't mean that new paradigms cannot replace old ones. From time to time they do, but never without a great struggle.

But it is not only our leaders who are incapable of helping us find a way out of the trap; those they are supposed to serve are, for the most part, wedded to the existing paradigm as well. They expect their leaders to solve unprecedented problems with methods designed to cope with the problems of the past.

To generate a massive escape from the trap, a universal grassroots movement is needed. Courageous women and men who have escaped from the trap themselves must take the risk to address the critical issues the present paradigm is incapable of solving. Above all, they must be motivated by a genuine desire to help others discover and develop their spiritual reality. Fortunately, we are beginning to see glimmerings of hope that such a movement is on the horizon. Through this and other programs of spiritual development, individuals are enabled to find the source of their goodness, learn how to tap into it, and use it in their interactions with others.

In chapter six we pointed out what happens to a person who commits a good deed, but we haven't mentioned what happens to recipients of the good deed. They are usually touched by an act of kindness and are moved to perform other acts of kindness themselves. Doing good is apparently contagious. While psychologists who have studied this phenomenon acknowledge that doing good inspires others to do good as well, they don't know what moves a person to respond in kind. Could it be that an act of goodness touches our souls and that the soul, which is the source of goodness, responds in the only way it can to what it knows is right by generating the desire to do something good?

To me, this dynamic is a reminder of our spiritual reality. Every human being is endowed with the means to act in a constructive, creative, and loving manner. We are not meant to lead the kind of life that most of us are forced to lead today. We are here for this earthly phase of our soul's journey so that we may know and love God, develop the virtues latent within us, and to do our part in helping to make the world a loving home for a united human family.

Those of us who have fled the trap are not only committed to rescuing those who remain trapped; we are also involved in helping to implement what God envisions for humanity. As we win our freedom, we become willing participants in the process of growth that is at work in the world today. We recognize that the twin processes of growth and decline are part of a greater evolutionary process that is destined to lead to the establishment of God's will for humanity. As we commit ourselves to gaining a more accurate understanding of reality and developing ourselves spiritually, we will be helping to draw closer to attaining that objective.

Imagine if most women and men and private and public institutions were to become involved in such an effort! Our communities would surely be safer, healthier, and happier places in which to live and work, because their citizens would be aware of their true selves and therefore happily involved in the spiritual development process. The social atmosphere and collective consciousness of the community would reflect love instead of hostility, trustworthiness instead of suspicion, faith instead of fear, humility instead of aggression. The community would be transformed, and the difficulties that plague us today would serve as a lesson of what can go wrong when we fail to rely on God.

I invite you to accept the challenge of spiritual development for yourself. You will not regret it.

Notes

Introduction

1. Bob Greene, *Springfield Union-News*, Dec. 19, 1992, p. 11.

Chapter 1

1. Bill Clinton (speech, Memphis, Tennessee, November 13, 1993).
2. A. M. Rosenthal, *Springfield Union-News*, Sept. 12, 1992.
3. Charles L. Whitfield, *Healing the Child Within* (audiocassette).

Chapter 2

1. Shoghi Effendi, *The Advent of Divine Justice*, p. 61.
2. Václav Havel, "The New Measure of Man," *The New York Times*, July 8, 1994, Op-Ed page.
3. Bahá'u'lláh, *Gleanings from the Writings of Bahá'u'lláh*, no. 117.1
4. Sultan Bin Salman al-Saud, quoted in Kevin Kelly, *Home Planet*.

Chapter 3

1. Thich Naht Hanh, *Being Peace*, p. 45.
2. 'Abdu'l-Bahá, *Some Answered Questions*, pp. 193–94.
3. Richard Morris, *The Edge of Science*, p. 5.
4. John Haller, *Outcasts from Evolution*, p. 4.
5. Fritjof Capra, *The Turning Point*, p. 47.
6. Ibid., p. 47.
7. Ibid., p. 86.
8. R. Buckminster Fuller, *Critical Path*, p. 55.
9. Peter Russell, *The Global Brain*, pp. 24–25.

10. Guy Murchie, *The Seven Mysteries of Life*, pp. 319–20.
11. Joan Borysenko, *Guilt is the Teacher, Love is the Lesson*, p. vii.

Chapter 4

1. Robbins Research International, *Living Health* (audiocassette).
2. Guy Murchie, *The Seven Mysteries of Life*, p. 345.
3. Ibid., p. 345.
4. Ibid., p. 351.
5. Jim Holt, "Anti Social Science?" *New York Times*, October 19, 1994, p. A23.
6. Guy Murchie, *The Seven Mysteries of Life*, p. 348.
7. Ibid., p. 351.
8. Ibid., p. 352.

Chapter 5

1. Scott M. Peck, *The Road Less Traveled* (audiocassette), "Part 3: Religion and Grace."
2. 'Abdu'l-Bahá, in *Paris Talks*, no. 15.7.
3. John Muir, *John of the Mountains*, p. 438.

Chapter 6

1. Scott M. Peck, *Further Along the Road Less Traveled*, pp. 95–96.
2. Guy Murchie, *The Seven Mysteries of Life*, p. 238.
3. Matthew Fox (interview with Polly Baumer), *Many Hands*, Spring, 1993, p. 5.
4. Elizabeth Kübler-Ross, *Working It Through*, p. 29.
5. Stephen R. Covey, *The Seven Habits of Highly Effective People*, p. 319.

Chapter 7

1. 'Abdu'l-Bahá, *Paris Talks,* no. 18.2.
2. Horace Holley, *Religion for Mankind,* p. 193.
3. Brenda Ueland, "Tell Me Now: On the Fine Art of Listening," *Utne Reader,* Nov./Dec., 1992, p. 7.
4. "Religion Could be the Key to Nation's Health," *Capitol-Statesman* (Madison, WI), April 11, 1993, Op-Ed page.
5. Elizabeth Kübler-Ross, *Death: The Final Stage of Growth,* p. 166.

Chapter 8

1. Nels Ferre, *The Sun and the Umbrella.* (The entire book is an explanation of the simile.)
2. Arnold Toynbee, *Surviving the Future,* p. 48.

Chapter 9

1. Pitirim Sorokin, *Social and Cultural Dynamics,* Vol. 4, p. 767.
2. H. M. Balyuzi, *Muḥammad and the Course of Islam,* pp. 287–310; Levy, *The Social Structure of Islam,* pp. 91, 98.
3. Pitirim Sorokin, *Social and Cultural Dynamics,* Vol. 4, p. 776.

Chapter 10

1. Udo Schaefer, *The Light Shineth in Darkness,* p. 10.
2. Horrace Holley, *Religion for Mankind,* p. 26.

Chapter 11

1. Bahá'í World Center Statistics Department, Haifa, Israel.

Chapter 12

1. Bahá'u'lláh, *Prayers and Meditations,* p. 272.
2. Nathan Rutstein, *He Loved and Served,* pp. 12–15.

Chapter 13

1. Bahá'u'lláh, *Gleanings from the Writings of Baha'u'llah*, no. 130.

Chapter 14

1. Scott M. Peck, *The Road Less Traveled* (audiocassette), "Part 3: Religion and Grace."
2. 'Abdu'l-Bahá, in *Star of the West*, Vol. 24, p. 350.
3. John Bradshaw, *Bradshaw on: The Family*, pp. 5, 12.
4. Bahá'u'lláh, *Tablets of Bahá'u'lláh*, p. 156.

Chapter 15

1. Larry Dossey, *Healing Words*, p. 149.
2. Alexis Carrel, *Man, the Unknown*, p. 47.
3. Bahá'u'lláh, *The Hidden Words*, Arabic, no. 5.
4. Shoghi Effendi, quoted in Ruth Moffett, *Du'á: The Call to Prayer*, pp. 30–32.

Chapter 16

1. 'Abdu'l-Bahá, in *Bahá'í Prayers*, pp. 174–75.
2. Bahá'u'lláh, *Gleanings from the Writings of Baha'u'llah*, no. 70.2.
3. 'Abdu'l-Bahá, quoted in Shoghi Effendi, *The Advent of Divine Justice*, ¶40.
4. Bahá'u'lláh, *The Hidden Words*, Arabic, no. 13.

Chapter 17

1. Bahá'u'lláh, in *Bahá'í Prayers*, p. 145.

Chapter 19

1. Bahá'u'lláh, in *Bahá'í Prayers*, p. 4.

Bibliography

Works of Bahá'u'lláh

Gleanings from the Writings of Bahá'u'lláh. new ed. Translated by
Shoghi Effendi. Wilmette, IL: Bahá'í Publishing, 2005.
The Hidden Words. Translated by Shoghi Effendi. Wilmette, IL: Bahá'í
Publishing, 2002.
Prayers and Meditations. 1st pocket-size ed. Translated by Shoghi
Effendi. Wilmette, IL: Bahá'í Publishing Trust, 1987.

Works of 'Abdu'l-Bahá

Paris Talks: 'Addresses Given by 'Abdu'l-Bahá in 1911. Wilmette, IL:
Bahá'í Publishing, 2006.
Some Answered Questions. 1st pocket-size ed. Translated from the
Persian by Laura Clifford Barney. Wilmette, IL: Bahá'í Publishing
Trust, 2004.

Compilations of Bahá'í Writings

*Bahá'í Prayers: A Selection of Prayers Revealed by Bahá'u'lláh, the Báb,
and 'Abdu'l-Bahá.* Wilmette, IL: Bahá'í Publishing Trust, 2002.
*The Divine Art of Living: Selections from the Writings of Bahá'u'lláh, the
Báb, and 'Abdu'l-Bahá.* Wilmette, IL: Bahá'í Publishing, 2006.

Other Works

Adler, Motimer J. *A Vision of the Future.* New York: Macmillan
Publishing, 1984.
Balyuzi, H. M. *Muḥammad and the Course of Islam.* Oxford: George
Ronald, 1976.
Barlett, Donald and James Steele. *America: What Went Wrong?* Kansas
City, KS: Andrews and McMeel, 1982.
Berry, Jason. *Lead Us Not Into Temptation: Catholic Priests and the
Sexual Abuse of Children.* New York: Doubleday, 1992.

Borysenko, Joan. *Guilt is the Teacher, Love is the Lesson: A Book to Heal You, Heart and Soul.* New York: Warner Books, 1990.

Bradshaw, John. *Bradshaw On: The Family.* Deerfield Beach, Florida: HCI, 1990.

Brown, Joseph Epes. *The Spiritual Legacy of the American Indian.* New York: Crossroad, 1992.

Capra, Fritjof. *The Turning Point.* New York: Bantam Books, 1982.

Carrel, Alexis. *Man, The Unknown.* New York: Harper and Row, 1935.

Carrol, Jackson. *As One with Authority: Reflective Leadership in Ministry.* Louisville, KY: Westminster/John Knox Press, 1991.

Cobb, John Jr., and David Griffin. *Process Theology: An Introductory Exposition.* Philadelphia, PA: Westminster Press, 1976.

Cousins, Norman. *In Place of Folly.* New York: Harper and Brothers Publishers, 1961.

Covey, Stephen R. *The Seven Habits of Highly Effective People.* New York: Simon & Schuster, 1989.

Dossey, Larry. *Healing Words: The Power of Prayer and the Practice of Medicine.* New York: Harper Collins Publishing, 1993.

Ferre, Nels. *The Sun and the Umbrella.* New York: Harper and Row, 1953.

Fuller, R. Buckminster. *Critical Path.* New York: St. Martins Press, 1991.

Haller, John Jr. *Outcasts of Evolution.* Champaign/Urbana, IL: University of Illinois Press, 1971.

Hanh, Thich Nhat. *Being Peace.* Berkeley, CA: Paralex Press, 1987.

Hoffman, David. *Bahá'u'lláh, The Prince of Peace.* Oxford: George Ronald, 1992.

Holley, Horace. *Religion for Mankind.* Oxford: George Ronald, 1956.

Kelly, Kevin W. *Home Planet.* Boston, MA: Addison Wesley Publishing Co., 1991.

Kübler-Ross, Elisabeth. *Working It Through.* New York: Macmillan Publishers, 1982.

————. *Death: The Final Stage of Growth*. Englewood Cliffs, NJ: Prentice-Hall, 1975.

Lebacqz, Karen and Ronald Barton. *Sex in the Parish*. Louisville, KY: Westminster/John Knox Press, 1991.

Lewontin, Richard C. *Human Diversity*. New York: Scientific American Library, 1982.

Levy, Reuben. *The Social Structure of Islam*. Cambridge: Cambridge University Press, 1965.

Loehle, Craig. *On the Shoulders of Giants*. Oxford: George Ronald, 1994.

McLuhan, Marshall and Bruce Powers. *The Global Village: Transformations in the World Life and Media in the Twenty-First Century*. New York: Oxford University Press, 1989.

McLuhan, Marshall and Edmund Carpenter. *Explorations in Communication*. Boston: Beacon Press, 1960.

Moffett, Ruth. *Du'á: The Call to Prayer*. Wilmette, IL: Bahá'í Publishing Committee, 1953.

Moody, Raymond Jr. *Life After Life: The Investigation of a Phenomenon, Survival of Bodily Death*. New York: Bantam Books, 1976.

————. *Reflections on Life After Life*. New York: Bantam Books, 1977.

Morris, Richard. *The Edge of Science*. New York: Prentice-Hall Press, 1990.

Muir, John. *John of the Mountains: The Unpublished Journals of John Muir*. Madison, WI: University of Wisconsin Press, 1979.

Murchie, Guy. *The Seven Mysteries of Life*. Boston: Houghton-Mifflin, 1978.

Peck, Scott M. *The Road Less Traveled*. Audiocassette. New York: Touchstone, 1986.

————. *Further Along the Road Less Traveled*. New York: Touchstone, 1994.

Russell, Peter. *The Global Brain*. Los Angeles: J. T. Tarcher, 1983.

Rutstein, Nathan. *Healing Racism in America: A Prescription for the Disease*. Springfield, MA: Whitcomb Publishing, 1993.

————. *He Loved and Served.* Oxford: George Ronald, 1982.

Sahtouris, Elisabet. *Gaia: The Human Journey from Chaos to Cosmos.* New York: Pocket Books, 1989.

Schafer, Udo. *The Light Shineth in Darkness: Five Studies in Revelation After Christ.* Oxford: George Ronald, 1977.

————. *The Imperishable Dominion.* Oxford: George Ronald, 1983.

Sears, William. *Thief in the Night.* Oxford: George Ronald, 1961.

Sorokin, Pitirim. *Social and Cultural Dynamics.* Vol. 4. New York: American Book Company, 1941.

Taherzadeh, Adib. *The Covenant of Bahá'u'lláh.* Oxford: George Ronald, 1992.

Toynbee, Arnold. *Surviving the Future.* New York: Oxford University Press, 1971.

Index

A

'Abdu'l-Bahá, 145
abusive parents, 155–56
adoption dream, 62
adultery, 197–200
Africa, 19
Africans, 25
AIDS, 6
alcohol addiction. *See* alcoholism
alcoholism, 9, 17
Alexander the Great, 101
American Indians, 25
American people
    great crisis of the spirit
      of, 5
ancient Greece, 24
anger instinct, 48
animals
    governed by physical
      instincts, 47
anxiety, 8
Aquinas, Thomas, 68
Archeology, 40
Aristotle, 24, 94
Asians, 25
atoms, 28
    interchange of, 37
attraction, power of, 37
Australia, 29

B

Bahá'í Faith, the, 114, 206
    discovery of, 157
Bahá'í writings, 133

Bahá'u'lláh, 113–16, 206, 207
    as divine educator, 114,
      123
    guidelines of, 115–16
    healing message of, 115
    on process of prayer, 164
    on self-knowledge, 148
    suffering of, 114, 115
    teachings of, 137
Baker Eddy, Mary, 94
Being Peace (Thich Nhat
    Hanh), 22
Bin Salman al-Saud, Sultan, 20
Bob, story of, 180–83
Bosnia, 30
Botha, N. C., 39
Buber, Martin, 87
Buddha, 94
    as divine educator, 123
Buddhism, 91
Burma, 93

C

Cambodia, 30
cancer, 6, 34
Capra, Fritjof, 28
Carrel, Alexis, 163
Ceasar, Julius, 101
Celts, 40
chastity, 199
child molestation, 2, 17
child rearing, 145–46
childbirth, 144
children, training of, 64

Christ, 90, 94
    return of, 110
    spiritual light of, 98
Christian sects, 110
Christianity, 91
Christians, 60, 88
Church, likened to an
    umbrella, 89
clergy, 50
Clinton, Bill, 5
Cold War, 6
collective consciousness,
    204–5
conscious mind, 144
conscious reality, 143
consciousness, 46
Continental Pipe Company,
    135
Córdoba, Spain, 101
creation
    as a single entity, 77
    structure of, 34
Creative Force, 52, 120, 178.
    See also God
Creative Word, 123
Creator, 52
    relationship with, 207
    See also God
crime, 140
critical mass, 205
Czech Republic, 14

D

Dalai Lama, 94
death, 54, 76–83
decay, 14
decline, process of, 218

deepening, 124, 125, 206
    definition of, 173
    as distinct from prayer,
    173
    importance of, 188
    likened to charging of a
    battery, 174
    likened to growing a
    flower, 175
    process of, 124, 182
    as source of inspiration,
    178
    as sustenance, 200
depression, 53
desires, fulfillment of, 197
despair, 53
devil, the, 25, 70n
diet, 130
disarmament treaties, 46
Discovery space shuttle, 20
Disraeli, Benjamin, 101
divine educators, 91–98,
    144
    carry out God's will,
    95
    guidance of, 131
    human side of, 94
    likened to mirrrors, 96
    likened to school
    teachers, 99
    message of, 100
    need for, 99–106
    purpose of, 97
    relationship with God,
    96
    as repositories of Holy
    Spirit, 97

as revealers of divine
laws, 196
source is God, 100
writings of, 125
divine guidance, 120, 196
divine laws, 150, 206
divine qualities, 75
divine revelation, 90
divine virtues, 63
development of, 204
Dobzhansky, Theodosius, 38
Dossey, Larry, 162
dreaming, 61–62
drug addiction, 9
drugs, 9, 140
dysfunctional communities, 199
dysfunctional families, 199

E

Earth
as one country, 30
atmosphere of, 31
economic barriers, 30
ego, 188
electrons, 21
Emerson, Ralph Waldo, 7
emotional abuse, 156
Encyclopaedia Britannica, 31
enlightenment, 59, 122
envy, 149
European Union, 19
Europeans, 25
evil, 61n, 109

F

faith, 149
false prophets, 108

false self, 18, 143–59
creation of, 157
development of, 155
dismantling of, 187
family, 149
breakdown of, 6, 48
fanaticism, 97
father
abuse of, 153
death of, 158
suicide attempt of, 154
fear, 8, 15
prevents hope, 15
Ferré, Nels, 88
Florida, 151
forgiveness, 192
free will, 48, 67, 120
freedom, 203
Fuller, Buckminster R., 27
Further Along the Road Less Traveled
(M. Scott Peck), 60

G

Gandhi, Mohandas, 87, 94
global civilization, 15
global economy, 30
global village, 29–30
God
authority of, 165
children of, 90
grace of, 132
guidance of, 173
intervention of, 93
knowledge of, 65, 121,
188
through divine
educators, 122

Bahá'í
PUBLISHING
and the Bahá'í Faith

Bahá'í Publishing produces books based on the teachings of the Bahá'í Faith. Founded over 160 years ago, the Bahá'í Faith has spread to some 235 nations and territories and is now accepted by more than five and a half million people. The word "Bahá'í" means "follower of Bahá'u'lláh." Bahá'u'lláh, the Founder of the Bahá'í Faith, asserted that He is the Messenger of God for all of humanity in this day. The cornerstone of His teachings is the establishment of the oneness of humankind, which will be achieved by personal transformation and the application of clearly identified spiritual principles. Bahá'ís also believe that there is but one religion and that all the Messengers of God—among them Abraham, Zoroaster, Moses, Krishna, Buddha, Jesus, and Muḥammad—have progressively revealed its nature. Together, the world's great religions are expressions of a single, unfolding divine plan. Human beings, not God's Messengers, are the source of religious divisions, prejudices, and hatreds.

The Bahá'í Faith is not a sect or denomination of another religion, nor is it a cult or a social movement. Rather, it is a globally recognized independent world religion founded on new books of scripture revealed by Bahá'u'lláh.

Bahá'í Publishing is an imprint of the National Spiritual Assembly of the Bahá'ís of the United States.

For more information about the Bahá'í Faith,
or to contact the Bahá'ís near you, visit

http://www.bahai.us/
or call
1-800-22-UNITE

Other Books Available from Bahá'í Publishing

The Ascent of Society
THE SOCIAL IMPERATIVE IN PERSONAL SALVATION
John S. Hatcher
$19.95 U.S. / $22.95 CAN
Trade Paper
978-1-931847-52-0

An illuminating examination of the relationship between individual spiritual development and the collective advancement of civilization.

In *The Purpose of Physical Reality* Dr. John S. Hatcher compared the physical world to a classroom designed by God to stimulate individual spiritual growth and to prepare us for birth into a spiritual existence. But how does personal spiritual development translate into social experience? Is there a social imperative connected with individual spiritual growth? Is involvement with others necessary for one to evolve spiritually? Hatcher analyzes these questions and more in *The Ascent of Society: The Social Imperative in Personal Salvation*. This penetrating study describes the objective of personal spiritual growth as an "ever-expanding sense of self" that requires social relationships in order to develop. Hatcher focuses on the Bahá'í belief that human history is a divinely guided process in which spiritual principles are gradually and progressively expressed in social institutions. He demonstrates that the aspirant to spiritual transformation cannot view personal health and development as being possible apart from the progress of human society as a whole.

John S. Hatcher holds a BA and an MA in English literature from Vanderbilt University and a PhD in English literature from the University of Georgia. He is the director of graduate studies in English literature at the University of South Florida, Tampa. A widely published poet and distinguished lecturer, he has written numerous books on literature, philosophy, and Bahá'í theology and scripture, including *Close Connections: The Bridge between Spiritual and Physical Reality, From the Auroral Darkness: The Life and Poetry of Robert E. Hayden, A Sense of History: The Poetry of John Hatcher, The Ocean of His Words: A Reader's Guide to the Art of Bahá'u'lláh,* and *The Purpose of Physical Reality.* He and his family live on a farm near Plant City, Florida.

Hidden Gifts
FINDING BLESSINGS IN THE STRUGGLES OF LIFE
Compiled by Brian Kurzius
$10.95 U.S. / $13.95 CAN
Trade Paper
978-1-931847-48-3

Have you ever wondered why we have problems and tests in our lives? Where do they come from? What is the most effective way to handle them? We may not see it, but there just might be a multitude of gifts hidden among our problems and tests.

In *Hidden Gifts: Finding Blessings in the Struggles of Life*, Brian Kurzius searches the Bahá'í scriptures for answers to the meaning of human suffering. What is the value of suffering in our lives? How do we decide on the best course of action? Are there qualities and attributes we can develop to help us more effectively face life's challenges? The answers to these questions and others are found in this spiritually edifying collection of extracts from Bahá'í scripture.

Over the course of many years, Brian Kurzius has studied the subject of human suffering extensively. His research increasingly drew him to the writings of the Bahá'í Faith on the subject. He now offers workshops and lectures frequently about finding gifts in the struggles of life. Kurzius is also the author of *Fire & Gold: Benefiting from Life's Tests*. Brian and his wife, Christine, live in Haifa, Israel, where they work for the Bahá'í World Center.

Religion on the Healing Edge
WHAT BAHÁ'ÍS BELIEVE
Frank Stetzer
$11.95 U.S. / $14.95 CAN
Trade Paper
978-1-931847-44-5

An introduction to the Bahá'í Faith that challenges readers to view religion, civilization, and spirituality in a new way.

Religion on the Healing Edge: What Bahá'ís Believe examines the defining beliefs animating the Bahá'í Faith and its distinctive practices, which are intended to change the world. Author Frank Stetzer offers insights into the Bahá'í community and its vision to establish a new global civilization based on the recognition of the oneness of humanity. The vision he presents is a bold and audacious one, full of unique opportunities and unusual challenges. A marvelous book for anyone interested in learning more about the mission of the Bahá'í Faith and the relevance of its teachings.

Frank Stetzer is a research statistician in the College of Nursing at the University of Wisconsin-Milwaukee. He holds a PhD in geography and an MS in statistics from the University of Iowa. Dr. Stetzer encountered the Bahá'í religion as a college student in the 1970s. He and his wife, Rosemary, have served in various capacities in several Bahá'í communities. They live in Wisconsin and enjoy the company of their three children.

The Secret of Divine Civilization
'Abdu'l-Bahá
$9.95 U.S. / $12.95 CAN
978-1-931847-51-3

An outstanding treatise on the social and spiritual progress both of nations and of individuals.

The Secret of Divine Civilization is a thorough explanation of the view of the Bahá'í Faith on the true nature of civilization. It contains an appealing and universal message inspiring world-mindedness and soliciting the highest human motives and attributes for the establishment of a spiritual society. Written by 'Abdu'l-Bahá in the late nineteenth century as a letter to the rulers and people of Persia, it is still profoundly relevant today as a guide to creating a peaceful and productive world.

'Abdu'l-Bahá, meaning in Arabic "Servant of the Glory," was the title assumed by 'Abbás Effendi (1844–1921), the eldest son and appointed successor of Bahá'u'lláh, the Prophet and Founder of the Bahá'í Faith. A prisoner since the age of nine, 'Abdu'l-Bahá shared a lifetime of imprisonment and exile with his father at the hands of the Ottoman Empire. He spent his entire life in tireless service to, and promotion of, Bahá'u'lláh's teachings.

To view our complete catalog,
please visit http://Books.Bahai.us

Printed in the United States
128352LV00003B/121-600/A